∞

From Atheism to Catholicism

From Atheism to Catholicism

Nine Converts Explain Their Journey Home

Edited by Brandon McGinley

With a Foreword by Marcus Grodi

EWTN PUBLISHING, INC.

Irondale, Alabama

EWTN Publishing, Inc.
5817 Old Leeds Road, Irondale, AL 35210

Distributed by Sophia Institute Press, Box 5284, Manchester, NH 03108

Library of Congress Cataloging-in-Publication Data

Names: McGinley, Brandon, editor.
Title: From atheism to Catholicism : nine converts explain their journey home / edited by Brandon McGinley ; with a foreword by Marcus Grodi.
Description: Irondale, Alabama : EWTN Publishing, Inc., 2017. | Includes bibliographical references.
Identifiers: LCCN 2017025197 | ISBN 9781682780343 (pbk. : alk. paper)
Subjects: LCSH: Catholic converts — Biography.
Classification: LCC BX4668.A1 F76 2017 | DDC 248.2/42 — dc23 LC record available at https://lccn.loc.gov/2017025197

First printing

∞

Contents

The Power of Conversion Stories

Marcus Grodi

I believe that there is nothing more miraculously powerful in this world than a conversion story. A prodigal son, who had received everything he had wanted, finds himself at the bottom of life, with no hope. Then Scripture tells us "he came to himself." In other words, grace had touched his heart and mind, when he was still lost at the bottom, so that he finally realized what his self-centeredness had wrought—and what he needed to do to come home (see Luke 15:11–25). A conversion story is miraculous because it points to the undeserved work of God's grace; and it is powerful because it has the capacity to be used by grace to change other people's lives.

By the grace of God, I, too, have my own story of conversion to Jesus Christ and His Church. Nearly twenty-five years ago, I started an apostolate called the Coming Home Network to help support people on the journey and to help them tell their stories of conversion in print and online. It was because of my work with this apostolate that Mother Angelica invited me to host the *Journey Home* program. For twenty years, as the host of this program, I have had the privilege of helping men and women tell their stories of how God has changed their lives—how He has led them to discover a deeper relationship with Jesus Christ, all the way home to His Catholic Church. These guests have come from all walks of life: clergy and laity; husbands, wives, parents, and grandparents; academics, doctors, politicians, and the rest of us regular folk; fallen-away Catholics, lifelong non-Catholics, and, as in this collection of conversion stories, atheists.

Scripture says in both the Old and New Testaments that not believing in a Creator God is a foolish thing. Psalm 53:1 states, "The fool says in his heart, 'There is no God.'" And St. Paul wrote to the Romans:

> Ever since the creation of the world [God's] invisible nature, namely, his eternal power and deity, has been clearly perceived in the things that have been made. So they are without excuse; for although they knew God they did not honor him as God or give thanks to him, but they became futile in their thinking and their senseless minds were darkened. Claiming to be wise, they became fools. (Rom. 1:20–22)

Well, there seems to be an increasing number of people who claim to have studied enough of the world to determine, at least for themselves, that there is no God—or at least that they have no need of a God to give meaning to their lives. And if the direction of our culture is any indication, a world without God does not seem to lead in the direction of hope.

How do we reach people who, "claiming to be wise," are so widely supported in today's cultural muck of relativism? Calling them "fools" and pointing to these Scriptures or to the *Catechism of the Catholic Church* doesn't usually help. How do we reach out to our children, siblings, and friends who have left the Church and wandered off into today's godless philosophies—especially when the witness of our own lives has not always been consistent? How do we reach that coworker whose life is falling apart around him, but whose past seemingly leaves no room for the consideration of God?

Herein lies the miraculous power of conversion stories. Actually, "stories" is the wrong term, for the nine accounts in this book are not fictional; rather, they are personal testimonies of how God, in His merciful love by grace, touched nine people, helping them to "come to their senses" and to see where vehemently denying God has taken them. As you read each account, you will discover that God's love for each unique person is, in itself, unique. He doesn't deal with every person in the same way, because we are all different; and yet, through the warp and weft of the fabric of these stories, you will see the same creative hand of our loving God.

When that prodigal son "came to himself," the working of grace also helped him to understand what he needed to do: return home, repent of his foolishness, and replace his pride with humility. This is one of the common threads of these stories, for none of the authors claim that it was their own wisdom or intelligence that awakened them to their plight; rather, it was the love of the Father. As the apostle John said so succinctly, "We love, because he first loved us" (1 John 4:19).

I hope you enjoy these stories, but more importantly I hope that they inspire you and challenge you to examine your life and to see where your own demands for freedom and self-sufficiency may have led you. I pray that these stories give you hope—that your children, siblings, and friends who have left the Faith may also, by the grace of God, find their way home. If God can bring the authors of this book home, He can bring anyone home! Our job is to pray, to love, and to witness.

∞

From Atheism to Catholicism

Chapter 1

Scatter the Darkness of My Mind

John L. Barger

Twenty-five and newly married, I was confronted daily by the religious claims of Susan, my bright, talented, Catholic wife, who was as baffled by my atheism as I was by her Catholicism.

Mind you, I had gone down the Christian road years before —or had tried to go down it—when I was just twelve and was baptized in the First Baptist Church of Handsboro, Mississippi. I left not long after because the boys told dirty jokes in Sunday school.

Religion, tainted by the odor of hypocrisy, faded from my life and was replaced by science, which, with its air of disinterested neutrality, offered me ever-growing certainty about facts of the material world. But by its nature science spoke not a word about the *meaning* of facts.

So, as a young man I plunged into the only serious thinkers I could find in the local library: Albert Camus, Jean-Paul Sartre, André Gide, and other existentialists. I stepped away from them feeling more unclean, grimmer, and more hopeless than ever.

From Atheism to Catholicism

To drink, then! And drugs, too! To seize a moment's pleasure and drive the dark away! Until the next morning, when, in the words of the great scholar and poet A. E. Housman, "I was I, my things were wet/the world it was the old world yet."

∞

"Explain to me, John," Susan said soon after our marriage began, "why in the black depths of the ocean, where light never penetrates, there are millions of brightly colored fish whose colors are never seen by any other living creature."

Beats me, I answered.

"Why," she persisted, "deep underground, where until recently no mine has ever penetrated, are there diamonds that would sparkle were there sunlight, and geodes whose brilliant crystals are entombed in stone so that nothing ever sees them—baubles that have lain there unappreciated for eons?"

I dunno.

"Why are there whales and whippoorwills, bears and butterflies, cats and caterpillars: lovely to the eye, charming to the soul, and themselves just a tiny portion of a cavalcade of fantastic creatures that swim the seas and crawl the earth?"

Why?

"I think," Susan answered, "it's because Something delights in beauty. And everywhere that that Something turns, it fills space with beautiful things—morning meadows and evening sunsets, mountain peaks and babies' dimples, and, of course, the moon and the stars that circle us every night. That Something is a profligate artist who paints with mad abandon, gracing creation with beauty seen and unseen, in every time and every place."

A Something? *Hmmph!*

∞

In those days, science was my touchstone. Susan urged me to pray for God's help; she insisted that He selflessly created us and even sacrificed Himself for us. I was sure, on the contrary, that "there ain't no such thing as a free lunch"—until I found out that science claims that there is such a thing as a free lunch.

Celebrated physicist Alan Guth said it all: "The universe is the ultimate free lunch."[1] About 13.7 billion years ago, according to modern physics, the whole shebang—matter, space, and even time—all surged into existence ... *out of nothing!*

That's about as free a lunch as you can get. And, said Susan, it's what the Church has said from the beginning. Aquinas asserted it in the 1200s, Augustine in the late 300s, and Genesis even earlier, sometime before 500 B.C.: The universe was created out of nothing.

Now, only a person whose sight is clouded (or who refuses to look) can fail to see what follows: Since matter, time, and space came from nothing, then something *outside of* matter, time, and space must have brought them into existence. Something, it seems, that loves beauty.

Exit atheism stage left. Or at least, it *should* exit.

But I am no St. Paul. With me, as with most people, conversion is a slow process, and it continues even today. Each new understanding is a modest light turned on in a vast, dark cavern. One light reveals the stalagmite nearby and another the wall on the left; a few more show the ceiling far above and suggest a path forward—but darkness yields only reluctantly. And half-light is not a satisfying prize.

---

[1] Steve Bradt, "3 Questions: Alan Guth on New Insights into the 'Big Bang,'" MIT News, March 20, 2014, http://news.mit.edu/.

From Atheism to Catholicism

∞

When I was in high school, a full ten years before I married Susan, I worked as a Red Cross Volunteer in the surgical lab of the local hospital. I helped prepare tissues for microscopic examination by the pathologist.

A number of times I assisted him with autopsies on tiny stillborn babies, some at only a few months' gestation. I can still see the details of those tiny beings, with their delicate hands and tiny toes, and, yes, their beauty—even in death. That summer I came to see the humanity of children in the womb, and I sorrowed for their deaths.

Ten years later and just nine months after Susan and I were married, the Supreme Court's 1973 *Roe v. Wade* decision mandated legal abortion nationwide. The decision crushed both of us: Susan because of her keen sense of justice and studied understanding of the Natural Law, and I because of my experience-based knowledge of the preciousness of unborn life.

Although I was not Catholic, I soon came to know and to admire the Church's unwavering anti-abortion stance even as public opinion turned against Her. Another light went on: The same institution that preached creation out of nothing treasured and defended the least and most helpless creatures in that Creation. But my eyes were still more accustomed to darkness than to the light.

∞

"I'll teach you a prayer," Susan said to me one day. "A prayer you can say without losing face. You don't even have to let me know you're saying it."

Lord Jesus Christ,
Son of the Living God,

I humbly beseech Thee
to scatter the darkness of my mind,
to give me lively faith, firm hope, and burning love.

Grant, O my God,
that I may come to know Thee well,
do all things in Thy light,
and in accordance with Thy holy will.

"If there's a God," she said, "I guarantee He'll answer. If not, what have you lost? Especially if you say it secretly."

Which I did each day as I drove to the Citadel, where, by then, I was a soldier taking classes. That summer, my rhetoric professor was Kent Emery, an intense young man who dosed the usually lightweight rhetoric classes with Plato, Aristotle, Augustine, and Aquinas. In class he quoted Frank Sheed, G. K. Chesterton, Hilaire Belloc, and even Cardinal Newman. To my chagrin, he claimed that there were truths more certain than my beloved science, which he argued only reveals the patterns of the material world—patterns that, though regular, are intrinsically frangible.

Regularity, he said, is not the same thing as necessity, and he demonstrated the point by telling a story adapted from the work of Bertrand Russell:

Every morning precisely at 6 a.m. the farmer's wife comes out to the chicken coop, steps in, and scatters feed for the chickens. One of the chickens is a scientist, and after months of seeing this sequence occur in exactly the same way every morning, he proposes a new Law of Nature: Just as the sun must rise every morning, so the farmer's wife must come out of the house at precisely 6 a.m. and feed us chickens.

All the other chickens are amazed at the scientist-chicken's sagacity and celebrate him for discovering a new Law of Nature ... until the day the farmer's wife comes out at 6 a.m. with an ax, grabs the scientist-chicken, chops off his head, and carries his headless corpse into the house to make chicken soup.

The scientist-chicken mistook the *regularity* of the lady's actions for *necessity*, just as most of us mistake the regularity of the motions and other properties of matter for necessity. In fact, we don't really know *why* the properties of the material world are as they are. For instance we know *that* gravity causes things to fall to Earth at thirty-two feet per second, rather than, say, thirty-eight feet per second, but we don't know *why* it does. Science uncovers and relies upon regularity, but it does not reach as far as necessity, which is the *only* realm in which absolute certainty can be found.

Kent's arguments shattered my absolute trust in science, but then he did something even more shocking: He revealed he was Catholic. And not merely Catholic but a daily communicant!

There are many ways to come to the door of the Church, but mine happened to be through ideas. From Kent, from his wife, from Susan, and from the authors whose books they now fed me—Cardinal Newman, St. Bonaventure, St. Augustine, St. Thomas Aquinas, Frank Sheed, C.S. Lewis, Christopher Dawson, and many others—answers and explanations tumbled so fast that within months, many more new lights had gone on in the darkness of my mind.

Chesterton's *Everlasting Man* showed me the essential difference between man and the animals, puncturing my confidence in the denuded secular understanding of evolution. C. S. Lewis's *Mere Christianity* and *The Abolition of Man* taught me the nature, reality, and reliability of the Natural Law. Christopher Dawson's *Making of Europe* showed the great contributions of the Church to Western culture. Étienne Gilson's *Spirit of Medieval Philosophy* retraced the decline of philosophy from the Middle Ages to the present, shoring up my confidence in the philosophical principles embraced by the Church.

Sigrid Undset's *Kristin Lavransdatter* showed me the nature of holiness in a fallen world, and Patricia Treece's *A Man for Others* showed me the face of actual holiness in our time: St. Maximilian Kolbe, who in Auschwitz freely gave his life for another. Thomas Merton's *Seven Storey Mountain* revealed to me the strength of silence and the power of prayer, and Thérèse of Lisieux's *Story of a Soul* shamed me for my pride and arrogance and sketched out the path I should tread: Pray more fervently the prayer that was already being answered: "Lord, scatter the darkness of my mind."

In less than a year, I was transformed from a confused, knee-jerk atheist into a seeker with an essentially Catholic mind. I had come to see the natural world as the Church sees it, as Her saints see it, as Christ sees it, and as God made it. Though people who met me accused me of being a hard-core Catholic, they were wrong: Having Catholic ideas does not yet a Catholic make. It's not enough to believe that what the Church teaches is true; you've got to come to believe that, by Her nature, the Church is a truth-teller. That step takes more than a revolution in ideas.

∞

"There were bugs everywhere," my father said, "and they got into our food. When we put sugar in our coffee, dead bugs floated to the top. We skimmed them off with a spoon." He was speaking of his time on Wake Island during World War II, and I believed what he said, even though I never saw those dead bugs or met anyone else who had seen them. Why? Because I knew from other experiences that my father did not lie—that is, I believed he was a truth-teller. And because I believed *in him as a truth-teller*, I believed *that what he said was true*, even in cases that were impossible for me to verify.

It's the same with the Church and the Faith. Because Catholics believe *in the Church as a truth-teller*, they believe *that what She says is true*, even in cases that are impossible to verify independently, such as the doctrine of the Trinity, the Real Presence of Christ in the Eucharist, and so forth. In turn, the Church affirms the teachings of Jesus because She believes *in Him as a truth-teller*. Well, more than that: She believes, as we are called to believe, that He is Truth itself.

But at this point in my journey I was still on the outside looking in. I held many Catholic ideas but did not acknowledge the Church to be, by Her very nature, a truth-teller. That gap can be bridged only by what is commonly called the "leap of faith," in which we go from *evidence-based* trust to *character-based* trust, in which we come to believe without direct evidence claims that the trusted person or entity asserts to be true.

In fact, we make such trusting judgments all the time, believing without direct evidence that the airline has fueled and properly maintained our plane, believing without direct evidence that the surgeon is competent to undertake the operation we are about to undergo, believing without direct evidence that our dinner is not laced with poison. In each case, we proceed in faith that is based on our belief in the trustworthy character of the entity with which we are dealing.

Why should it be different for the Church? Those who approach Her with humility come to see for themselves the truth of the claims She makes about virtue and vice, human life, and the world we live in. In my case, I came to see that the Church spoke truthfully about abortion; She spoke truthfully about marriage; and She spoke truthfully about many other controversial aspects of the world and of human experience that I could independently verify, particularly when it came to the Natural Law. Indeed in these cases, I found Her *never to speak falsely*.

At a certain point, therefore, I came to see the Church not merely as an entity that held views I knew to be true; I came to see Her as a truth-teller. That is, I came to have faith in Her intrinsic veracity, both about things I could and could not verify myself.

Now, all this sounds quite linear, like a complicated math problem in which one result led me logically to the next, with the final conclusion emerging from the steps that came before. But the truth is that something deeper than and fundamentally different from logic is also needed for true conversion: the shedding of pride and its resistance to authority outside itself.

∞

"Lord, Jesus Christ, Son of the living God," Susan taught me to pray, "scatter the darkness of my mind."

That's a simple phrase, but when prayed genuinely it packs a wallop. It requires of the supplicant a number of transformational attitudes: first, acknowledgment that darkness may afflict his mind; second, admission that he may need help in dispelling that darkness; and third, acceptance of the fact that there may be a Being greater than himself Who can help him to do so. All three of these stances are obviously incompatible with knee-jerk atheism. Indeed, each is an essential admission that must be made if ever the darkness is to be scattered.

In genuinely praying that prayer, I took all three steps—and if you are an atheist who genuinely seeks the truth, so must you, or you are living a lie.

I had opened a door, and God walked in—by means of Susan, whose faith no longer baffled me; by means of Kent and his wife, whose conversation opened my mind; and by means of the many Catholic authors whose writings were finally making sense of the confusing and dark world I had inhabited for so many years. Inevitably, therefore, I was pushed past my newfound Catholic ideas to the essential question: Is the Church more than a repository of true ideas? Is She essentially a truth-teller whose words can be trusted when She speaks of things about God that no human person can directly verify?

In other words: Could I move beyond "I see" to "I believe"? Was there a way for me to find "lively faith, firm hope, and burning love?"

∞

I always thought divine revelation to be unlikely until I mused on how I talk to my pets. Of course they hardly understand a thing, but we address them as if they did—and we'd be delighted if they fully understood us and would respond to us, telling us about their day and how they're feeling and what they desire or need.

It seems to me that even though our pets can know but little of our interior lives and the meaning of what we say, our conversations with pets are natural. And it seems to me, then, that God's efforts at communication with us are just as natural, even though we can grasp but little of His interior life and the meaning of His words. Indeed, to me, *not speaking* to pets is stranger than speaking to them; and similarly, God's *not speaking* to us seems stranger than His speaking to us.

If there is a God, the fact of revelation makes more sense to me than its absence would. Indeed, an honest, inquiring atheist should look around for revelations, expecting that if there is a God, He would seek to speak to us.

And when we look, that's exactly what we find. Jewish history records thousands of years of claims that God has spoken directly to individuals — claims not made by the gullible or the insane, but by many of the sanest and wisest of the Jewish people: Abraham, David, Solomon, Moses, Isaiah, Job, and scores of other men known, even apart from their commerce with God, as brilliant thinkers, wise leaders, and men whose eloquence was the envy of the generations.

Although His speaking directly to me would be an answer to my prayer — "Grant, O my God, that I may come to know Thee well" — as of this writing He still has never said a word to me at all — directly, at least. That's His choice.

And my faith in Him is mine.

The Church claims to speak infallibly in certain restricted matters. Either She has justification in making that claim, or She is one of the proudest, most mendacious of entities on Earth. The same can be said, of course, about Christ's claim that He is God. If there is no justification for these claims, then we must reject both the Church and Christ.

But when we look at the many saints who have arisen from the Body of Christ, we find in them not pride but profound humility, not greed but great generosity, not mendacity but gentle truthfulness — sometimes even at the costs of their lives.

From Atheism to Catholicism

In discovering the Church to be right in so many areas where I could verify Her claims, and in seeing the virtues that blossom in those who follow Her teachings, I found it impossible to believe Her to be the proud, mendacious caricature presented by Her enemies. And so I had to choose either to accept the Church as a divinely founded, divinely protected institution or to step away entirely.

I chose to believe in the Church and to accept on faith Her teachings about Jesus and about other divine matters beyond my knowledge and understanding. I came to see Her as a virtuous institution that speaks truly; I came to believe *in Her as a truth-teller*.

∞

Now, what about you?

Have you genuinely considered the teachings of the Church, seeking to understand them authentically on their own terms? Having done so, can you name any institution that has greater claim to being a truth-teller about things eternal?

And once you come to see that the Church is not merely right about many things but is Herself a truth-teller, do you have the humility to acknowledge that fact publicly and enter the fold?

But I ask too much, too soon. Let me ask instead whether you can admit that there is in your mind darkness mixed with light—some uncertainty about whether you have perfectly apprehended the nature of the universe. If you can't make that measly admission, you're living a lie and will never come to see the truth. If, however, you can simply acknowledge that some darkness taints your mind, you have taken the first step and are, in fact, well on your way.

∞

Susan died of cancer just after she turned forty. She spent her last few days consoling and encouraging those who were suffering her imminent loss. If death can be holy, hers was. She prayed for me before she died, and I believe that since that dread day in 1987, she has continued to intercede for me.

I believe, as well, that if you pray with me now, she will intercede for you, too, and will help you to develop lively faith, firm hope, and burning love. Whether you are already Catholic or just an inquirer, I invite you to join me. Do it in private if you must, but I urge you to do it, and do it now. Today and every day, pray with me:

> Lord Jesus Christ,
> Son of the Living God,
> I humbly beseech Thee
> to scatter the darkness of my mind,
> to give me lively faith, firm hope, and burning love.
>
> Grant, O my God,
> that I may come to know Thee well,
> do all things in Thy light,
> and in accordance with Thy holy will.

God bless you, and welcome to the Catholic Church!

Chapter 2

Further Up and Further In

Holly Ordway

How did I ever end up in the Catholic Church? I certainly never expected to arrive here. As an atheist English professor, I never imagined that I'd become a Christian, but greatly to my own surprise, I did. Then, having been baptized at the age of thirty-two, I thought I had "arrived." I had found my place, as an Episcopalian in the conservative Anglo-Catholic tradition—but definitely not a Catholic, thank you very much! And so I would have been bemused at best, or more likely unsettled or even horrified, by the thought of myself today, not just a Catholic, but also beginning my day by praying the Rosary in front of a tabletop statue of Our Lady of Fatima. A devotion to Mary? What? No!

So it has indeed been quite a journey, from atheism to faith, then all the way Home into the Catholic Church—and then "further up and further in" as I grow in faith as a Catholic.

I was raised in a nonreligious family. We never went to church; there was no Bible in the house; and with the awkward exception of Grace said at Thanksgiving (and no other time), there was no mention (much less discussion) of God at all. The result was that I knew nothing whatsoever about what it meant to be a Christian, but I also wasn't hostile—merely uninformed and indifferent. I remember a conversation I had when I was about eight years old. A classmate asked me if I believed in God. I replied, "I don't know. Maybe God's real, maybe not." The boy said "Oh, you're an agnostic then." I was happy to have learned a new vocabulary word, but the larger question of the existence of God made no impression on me at all. In my teens, I began to be concerned with questions of right and wrong, and I felt a longing for meaning and connection, but it didn't occur to me to explore these issues in religious terms.

My family was nonetheless "culturally Christian" in a very small way: At Christmas, there were Christmas carols on the record player, and a Nativity scene on a side table. As a little girl, I was fascinated by that Nativity set. I would play with it, moving the little sheep closer to Baby Jesus. I didn't know what it meant, and no one ever explained it to me, but it was attractive in a mysterious way. It planted a sort of imaginative seed.

More seeds of faith were planted by my reading. I was a very bookish girl. (Indeed, I'm a bookish adult!) I devoured all the reading material I could get my hands on. Significantly, I read C. S. Lewis's Chronicles of Narnia and found these stories tremendously gripping—though I had no idea they were about Jesus. And I read J. R. R. Tolkien's *Lord of the Rings*, which became the creative work that has most shaped my life. In retrospect, I see that God's grace was working there in my imagination, but it would not bear fruit for many years yet.

In college I absorbed the prevailing idea that religion in general, and Christianity in particular, was just a historical curiosity and that science could explain everything. By my mid to late twenties, I was firmly an atheist. I did not believe I had a soul; rather, I thought I was just an intelligent animal and that when

I died my consciousness would simply blink out. I thought that there was no ultimate meaning in life and that people who believed in any form of God were seriously self-deluded. It was depressing, but I believed it to be the best explanation of the way the world is, and truth is better than false comfort.

Yet certain things got under my skin. For one thing, rather annoyingly, I felt that it was important to try to be a good person—but as an atheist, I couldn't explain why. I knew as surely as I knew anything that it was wrong to hurt someone without a good reason, and that it was better to be kind than to be cruel. But *why* should I have a sense of morality separate from my own self-interest?

I tried to figure out justifications. Perhaps, I thought, what we call a conscience is simply a recognition that society is better off if we help each other. Unfortunately, that doesn't really account for why we should *self-sacrificially* care for anyone else. I could say that morality must be useful for the survival of the species, so it must therefore have evolved. But this is simply begging the question; evolution became the rug under which I tried to sweep all my questions about meaning. Just because one might be able to create a natural-selection just-so story for something, that doesn't make that story true.

I believed it was important to be intellectually honest (another scruple that couldn't be explained by my atheism), so I had to admit that I didn't have an adequate explanation for my own moral sense, nor for my desire for meaning in my life, nor for my appreciation of beauty. But at that point, I would not have even considered looking to Christianity for possible answers. I thought that faith was just "blind faith"—deliberately believing things contrary to reason to make yourself feel better. I couldn't do that then—and I still can't. So, given what I thought faith was, I didn't bother to investigate it.

From Atheism to Catholicism

The other thing that was running against the grain of my materialist worldview was literature. Lewis and Tolkien had given me, as a child, a glimpse of a reality more meaningful than just what I could see and touch. Then, in college, I majored in English literature. I am grateful to have had a solid literary education; in reading the classic authors, I discovered that so much of great English literature is deeply Christian. I read the Anglo-Saxon poets, Chaucer, Shakespeare, John Donne, T. S. Eliot, Gerard Manley Hopkins, and so on; their work resonated with me, especially the Catholic poet Hopkins. I didn't follow up on their faith for many years, but their writing was eroding my atheist assumptions.

Then I did a strange, even paradoxical thing: As a convinced atheist, I did my doctoral work on fantasy literature and centered it on the writings of J. R. R. Tolkien—a devout Catholic. I could have done my dissertation on a variety of literary topics, but I chose fantasy, and I chose Tolkien because I went for what was *meaningful*, even though I didn't think it was *true*. My experience was like that of C. S. Lewis, who commented that at one point in his life, "nearly all that I loved I believed to be imaginary; nearly all that I believed to be real I thought grim and meaningless."[2] My imagination had been fed and nourished by Tolkien, this great Catholic author; yet I was still holding him at arm's length.

Finally, it was the poets who tipped the balance. Rereading classic Christian poetry in preparation for teaching it—by now I had gotten my Ph.D. and become a teacher of English literature—I found myself unwillingly intrigued. I did not want to become a Christian, but I had finally admitted that I couldn't dismiss these writers' faith as something stupid or trivial. You

---

[2] C. S. Lewis, *Surprised by Joy* (New York: Harcourt, Brace, Jovanovich, 1966), 170.

can disagree with Tolkien, Donne, Hopkins, or Eliot, but you can't call them stupid or uneducated! Eventually, I came to the conclusion that this thing called faith might be a little more complex and interesting than I was giving it credit for.

The Christian writers did more than pique my interest about the true meaning of faith. Books such as *The Lord of the Rings* had given me a glimpse of a different view of the world—one that was richly meaningful and beautiful and also made sense of both the joy and the sorrow, the light and the dark that I saw and experienced. My atheist view of the world was, in comparison, narrow and flat; it could not explain why I was moved by beauty and cared about truth. The Christian claim might not be true, I thought to myself, but it had a depth that was worth investigating.

Well, I started asking questions—and God had me right where He knew I needed to be.

∞

I'm retired from the sport now, but I was a competitive fencer for nearly twenty years. Around the time I started my new teaching job, I had also found a top-notch fencing club and coach. After working with my coach for about a year, I was surprised to learn that he was a Christian. He was an exemplary coach—very patient, intelligent, and thoughtful—and thus he challenged my stereotypes about Christians being pushy and thoughtless. So, when I became curious about what Christians really believe—when poetry had done its work!—I realized that I could feel safe and respected while discussing this topic with him. I asked a lot of questions, and I argued, and I read a great deal—and I became convinced on rational grounds that God exists.

What convinced me? It wasn't a single argument all by itself; there is no silver bullet in apologetics. Rather, it was the connecting of different pieces into a coherent overall argument. For one thing, there was the question of existence. Everything that comes into existence has a cause; one can trace it back, and back, and back, but eventually one has to ask: How did creation *itself* come to be? The best and only truly satisfactory answer is that there is Something that—or *Someone who*—is self-sufficient, not contingent like all the rest of creation. This being was not the "god" I had imagined as a skeptic: an old man in the sky like the popular image of Zeus. No, that idea of God was just as silly and unbelievable as I had thought. Rather, this God, the Creator, is—as I would later learn was articulated so well by St. Thomas Aquinas—the Ground of All Being, in fact Being Itself, the great I AM.

And the existence of this I AM—a different *kind* of being from anything in the created order—made sense of my moral intuition as well. I have no patience with those who say that atheists cannot be moral or do good. Of course they can and they do, and recognizing this doesn't alter the claims of Christianity. What atheism can't provide is a convincing account of why goodness matters and where it comes from; moreover, it can't supply the remedial help needed when we go wrong. What the Church offers us, which we can obtain nowhere else, is personal knowledge of the very source of goodness, plus salvation when we screw up, as we inevitably will—a salvation that consists not only in eternal life after we die, but in supernatural aid to our faith, hope, and love during our earthly lives. As an atheist, I failed badly in many respects, but I couldn't account for why my conscience troubled me. But if the very Creator Himself was Goodness, Truth, and Beauty, then I could understand why it was that I had this moral sense so deeply ingrained, and why I had recognized its claims even before I had faith.

Believing in God did not make me a Christian, but it made me want to follow up on the Christian claims. Why Christianity and not any other religion? Why not simply be "spiritual" without the nuisance of religious doctrine? I investigated Christianity because Christianity made a specific claim, one that could be investigated as any other historical claim: the Resurrection. If the Resurrection happened, then Christianity is true. St. Paul himself said that if Christ had not been raised from the dead, then Christian faith was in vain (see 1 Cor. 15:17). That is a bold statement!

So I decided to investigate, thinking that I would discover that you had to just take the Resurrection on faith and that there wasn't really any evidence. Then I did my research — and much to my surprise, I realized that there *is* evidence. After looking at it long and hard from many angles, I was convinced: The Resurrection had really happened.

My academic studies in literature allowed me to recognize that the Gospels were written as history, not myth or parable, and that there hadn't been enough time between the events and their written records for a legend to form. My knowledge of human psychology told me something about the behavior of the disciples: When Jesus was arrested, they deserted Him, and after the Crucifixion, they gave up and went away, assuming He was a failed messiah. If the disciples had made up the Resurrection story afterward, why would they have included details that made them look disloyal and cowardly? Then, after the Resurrection, they become bold proclaimers of the Risen Lord. There were plenty of words that people in ancient times could have used to describe visions of ghosts, and indeed such language would have gotten them in much less trouble! But they spoke of a Jesus who was alive — bodily resurrected — and in short order they were willing to die for that claim—not something they would have done for a lie of their own concocting.

Perhaps the most convincing evidence for the Resurrection, though, was the Church. If I supposed that the Church had invented the Resurrection to explain Her own worship of Jesus, I had to ask, how did that worship arise in the first place? If the Church were not the result of a miracle, She was Herself a miracle.

Even after I was convinced that the Resurrection had happened, I realized that I was struggling with the idea of the Incarnation. How could it be that the God Who created the galaxies became man? My intuition guided me here. I realized that I needed to reread *The Chronicles of Narnia*. And in the figure of Aslan, the Great Lion, I saw a picture of the Incarnate Lord, powerful and majestic, but touchable, real, and embodied. And, somehow, by re-encountering Aslan in *The Lion, The Witch, and the Wardrobe* and in *The Horse and His Boy*, I found that it made sense: I realized that this is what it would be like for God to become man. And I was ready to accept Christ as Lord.

What then? I said the typical evangelical sinner's prayer, began trying to live out the Christian faith, and discovered right away that simply committing yourself to Christ doesn't make you perfect. I started going to a conservative Episcopal church, where I was baptized on the feast of St. Michael and the Angels (perfect for a fencer!). I was well-discipled, and I immediately appreciated the liturgical worship, which helped me to begin to learn how to pray. (I say "begin" because I have realized, as a Catholic, how much more depth there is to prayer than I ever thought!)

I spent six years as an Episcopalian, thinking of myself as an Anglican. And I was quite happy there.

∞

God really has a great sense of humor, because, not only did He take me from being an unbeliever to becoming a Christian, but He took me from being a Episcopalian English professor to becoming a Catholic apologist teaching at Houston Baptist University. Talk about things that you don't see coming!

At that time, I viewed Anglicanism as the best of all possible worlds. I could take all the décor and the furnishings from the Catholics. I could adopt their devotional practices, omitting the ones that made me uncomfortable (such as anything that had to do with Mary). I could appreciate their art and their sense of history. It had all the benefits and none of the obligations. I was free to pick and choose. It was really gratifying, and I was quite happy to be an Anglican—except that I began to realize that the Anglican church was not coherent on a number of issues.

Take sexual ethics, for instance. I had gone from being very strongly pro-abortion as an atheist, to being staunchly pro-life. But in the Episcopal church, it's actually a bit dicey to be strongly pro-life. Once, after I had spoken strongly against abortion during a Sunday-school lecture at my church, the pastor drew me aside and said, "Don't press the pro-life issue. It will distress some people." I knew he was trying to do what was best for his parishioners, but it disturbed me: How could we truly help people if we aren't free to say, even in church, that abortion is wrong?

And then there was the question of women priests. Now, when I became a Christian, I wrestled with this question. Many people assumed that because I was excited about apologetics, I would eventually be ordained. The Episcopal church is very open to women clergy; even now some of the breakaway Anglican groups are too. But, in doing my research, I realized that the Church throughout history has had, and taught, a male-only priesthood. Jesus Himself chose twelve male apostles even though He had women whom He could have selected for the role. Was I going to second-guess Our Lord, and say that the Son of God bowed to the cultural pressures of His day and didn't choose women apostles, even though that meant that two thousand years would go by before His Church figured out what He really wanted?

The question is not whether women are being denied power by an oppressive Church. To begin with, it is a fundamentally secular approach to treat the priesthood as if it were just another ministry position, and it is a fundamentally modern secular approach to consider the priesthood in terms of power. Furthermore, my academic background includes medieval literature and history, and I knew full well that women do not need to be priests to have significant roles in the Church. I had read of abbesses, queens, scholars, mystics, founders and reformers of religious orders, even advisers to bishops and Popes: women such as St. Hilda of Whitby, St. Margaret of Scotland, St. Catherine of Siena, St. Teresa of Avila, Julian of Norwich—and the list goes on. And, of course, though I would not have admitted it at the time, there is, above all, Mary, the Mother of God.

As a woman, I realized that these calls for women priests, against the universal practice and teaching of the historic Church, were actually *contrary* to a full affirmation of women's value. Women have their own gifts and their own role in the Church, distinct from men's; if that's considered somehow lesser than men's roles, the proper response is to affirm the value of women's contributions, not to try to push women into men's roles, as if men's roles were the only important ones! As a scholar and a teacher, I have equal authority in my field and in my work as a male scholar and teacher does; this does not make me the *same* as a man, nor do I wish that it would.

So I came to the conclusion, after my research and reflection, that women could not be priests (not *should not*, but *cannot*). But the Episcopal church in the United States, and the Church of England in the United Kingdom, said otherwise. This left me wondering: How do these churches have the authority to change the very nature of the priesthood? The church that I attended at that time didn't have any women clergy, so I was able to dodge the issue, but it remained an irritating and unresolved issue.

And it was a significant unresolved issue, because it was the first hint of my deepest problem with Protestantism: the question of authority.

∞

My first inkling of this problem came as I began a second master's degree in apologetics at a thoroughly Protestant university. I had no particular arguments with the Protestants when I went in — but I did when I came out!

I have an orderly mind. Every time a doctrinal topic came up, my professors naturally taught the Protestant view; for the sake of completeness, I decided to find out what my own Anglican church said; and what the Orthodox said; and what the Catholics said. I found time and again that the Catholics made the most sense — in particular, with regard to Scripture.

We all took as a given that the Bible is true, inerrant, and inspired by God. This was no mere devotional or history book, but God's written Word, communicated through human authors. But how did we know that to be *true*? It doesn't do to say that Scripture itself says that it is the Word of God. Any book can say anything. Why should we *trust* it?

From Atheism to Catholicism

The Protestant position, insofar as I understood it, did not seem to present a clear answer. At best, it seemed, we were to use our own reason to assess the evidence and then come to agree that Scripture is inspired and inerrant. But, as the example of Martin Luther shows, this puts previously uncontested books, such as the epistle of St. James, up for debate.

On the other hand, the Catholic position was logical, historical, and definitive. We could trust the Bible because the Church had declared it to be trustworthy. And we could trust the Church because She was directly founded by Jesus Christ, who is Her Head, and because She is guided by the Holy Spirit, working through the apostles—commissioned by Jesus Christ Himself—and through their successors, the bishops. Christ first gave us Himself, and then He gave us His Church; it is only through His Holy Church that we have His Holy Word, for it was the early members of the Church who wrote that Word! We can trust it because we can trust them.

But then I had to work out what it really means to "trust the Bible." It's all very well to say that the Bible has no errors—but no errors *in what sense*? After all, when Jesus says, "I am the vine" (John 15:5), He is not to be understood literally. I was now up against the problem of the *interpretation* of Scripture. It became obvious that the right interpretation of Scripture is *not* plainly evident from a simple reading of the text, because I could see intelligent, well-educated, devout Christians coming to different points of view. My Protestant brothers and sisters did not disagree only with the Catholics; they also disagreed among themselves, getting different answers out of the same Scripture. This was deeply unsettling.

I am an academic, a literary critic, and a poet; I am quite comfortable with (and, if I may say so, reasonably skilled at) interpreting and analyzing texts. Perhaps because of that, I'm aware of the limits of certainty in this discipline. I was always left with the nagging question: What grounds did I have for believing *my* opinion to be correct? To be sure, I could go to this or that commentary on Scripture, written by well-qualified scholars, but how would I choose which commentary to rely on? How would I decide, say, between Martin Luther and Thomas Aquinas? In order to choose Luther rather than Aquinas, I would have to agree already with the Protestant position — but on what basis?

In fact, the more I thought about it, the more the question of authority seemed to loom far above all other issues. Was it really true that I was the ultimate arbiter of the truth? It was easy to say no, but deferring authority to commentaries and scholars whom *I* chose by my own criteria was just a shell game, to hide the blatant individualism of my faith. These were unsettling questions, but I put them on the back burner. I just didn't want to think too much about the issue.

God had other ideas.

∞

I had been considering a shift into more specifically Christian teaching, and out of the blue I was invited to build — and teach in — a brand-new cultural apologetics program at Houston Baptist University. I had never even heard of HBU until then! Accepting this position meant going out on a limb: I had tenure at my college in California, and I had to sell my house. But I saw very quickly that this was a once-in-a-lifetime opportunity — good, important, exciting work.

I took the job. My work started in the fall, so over the summer, which I spent in Oxford, England, I began thinking about where I would go to church in Houston. Very quickly I realized that I would have to make compromises if I were to stay in the Episcopal church.

I recognized the central issue one day when I was sitting in the Anglican church of St. Mary Magdalen and heard the priest talk about the Church of England's impending decision regarding the ordination of female bishops. (The Episcopal church in the United States already had female bishops, but I had been doing my best to ignore the fact.) This brought my question about authority to a head. One can more or less ignore the issue of female priests by thinking of them as ministry leaders, but bishops are different: They not only preach and teach (and celebrate the Eucharist), but they ordain other priests.

One can make some (weak) arguments in favor of women priests based on the women who are mentioned in Scripture as helping in the early Church, but never have there been any women bishops at any time in Church history. So how can the Church of England or the Episcopal Church decide in the twenty-first century to make women bishops? And if I *don't* believe that women can be priests, but I *do* think that the Church has authority, then how could I be in a church that has women bishops? How can authority be real if I pick and choose when to accept it?

I was all in a tangle. Then God pulled a divine trick on me. I was talking to a friend of mine, an Anglican, chatting about his writing and about what was going on in the Church of England. And he said, "I'm going to become a Catholic." Without even thinking of it, I immediately replied, "I'm headed toward Rome too." I thought: "What have I just said? Where did that come from?" As soon as I said it, though, I knew it was true. It had been surprised out of me; I hadn't expected his announcement, and I hadn't anticipated my reaction.

All of a sudden, I realized that my conscience had arrived at Rome before the rest of me, and that I just had to catch up.

I spent quite an interesting period wrestling with the issues, talking with my Catholic friends, looking at the Scriptures again with new eyes, and seeing that everything makes sense if Peter really is the Vicar of Christ, the visible head of the Church. As Jesus said: "You are Peter, and on this rock I will build my church, and the powers of death shall not prevail against it. I will give you the keys of the kingdom of heaven, and whatever you bind on earth shall be bound in heaven, and whatever you loose on earth shall be loosed in heaven" (Matt. 16:18–19).

Everything started to cohere at last. It is in the Church that everything fits together, for, as Jesus says, "I am with you always, to the close of the age" (Matt. 28:20). He didn't leave us alone, helplessly trying to figure out what the Bible says. He is still with us, by His Spirit, present in the Church, guiding us to all truth. Truth no longer depended just on *my* interpretation.

But, of course, the scary thing about this realization was that it meant I was no longer in charge. If, as I had realized, the Catholic Church has the only legitimate claim to ultimate authority, derived from Our Lord Jesus Christ Himself, then I had to come to terms with what the Church taught.

Among other things, that included coming to terms with Mary. I soon realized that the problem wasn't that Catholics had too high a view of Mary; rather, I had too low a view of *Jesus.* Mary isn't just one woman among many; she is the *Mother of God*, and therefore her flesh and blood formed Jesus' body. The commandment says "Honor your mother and your father," and so, of course, Our Lord honors His Mother! How can I do less? It would take me much longer to understand Mary's place in the Church, and to appreciate her, but I realized that I could no longer use her as an excuse to stay outside the Church.

I started going to Mass in Oxford, though not receiving Communion, of course. I had been to a Catholic Mass just once before. Now, there in Oxford, I had a profound recognition that this is real—that this is where the Lord is.

∞

I thought I had laid down my arms once and for all when I became a Christian, but I discovered that I was still holding my own, saying in effect, "I want to be the one who decides about doctrine." Finally I had to say, "Lord, I'm going to lay down my arms completely. The Church is the Church. Here is true authority. This is Home. I want to come Home." And so I did.

C. S. Lewis, who was and is hugely important in my life and work, never became a Catholic. One of his reasons was the authority of the Church. He wrote:

> The real reason why I cannot be in communion with you is not my disagreement with this or that Roman doctrine, but that to accept your Church means, not to accept a given body of doctrine, but to accept in advance any doctrine your Church hereafter produces. It is like being asked to agree not only to what a man has said but to what he's going to say.[3]

Lewis was quite right in identifying this as a key issue. From a Protestant perspective, it seems madness to accept, in advance,

[3] C. S. Lewis, "Christian Reunion: An Anglican Speaks to Roman Catholics," in *C. S. Lewis Essay Collection and Other Short Pieces* (New York: HarperCollins, 2000), 396.

all the potential claims that an organization might make. For instance, as far as I can tell, most Protestants object to the dogma of the Assumption of Mary—but not on theological grounds. Rather, they object to the Church's asserting something as truth to be accepted by the faithful, rather than something to be considered and accepted or rejected by each individual. It is the authority, not the dogma, that is at issue.

The key insight, however, is this: The Church is not a purely human organization, even though it is composed of ordinary, fallible, sinful human beings. It is, most truly, Christ's Body, animated by His Spirit; it is the extension through space and time of His Incarnation. And against this Body, He told us, the gates of hell will not prevail (see Matt. 16:18). The Church's authority, then, is Christ's authority. Our willingness to accept Church teaching is the test of our obedience to Christ.

But this is not chiefly a matter of obeying laws; it is a matter of believing in Love. The Church is the Bride of Christ. If marriage is what the Church has always taught it is—permanent, sacramental, faithful, fruitful—then to marry means to accept, in advance, whatever demands may come in the future, from spouse or children: "For better, for worse, for richer, for poorer, in sickness and in health" (as the Anglican Book of Common Prayer has it). One hasn't truly married if one reserves the right to accept or reject the proper fruit of that marriage. And if this is so even in ordinary marriages, how much more so in the mystical union of Christ and His Church?

The Church is the Body of Christ, of which Our Lord is the Head—not in a metaphorical way, but in a real way. The Church's teaching is the teaching of Our Lord. If we were present among Jesus' disciples during His earthly ministry, we would be called on to follow Him. We would not be truly following

Him unless we accepted, in advance, all that Our Lord would teach—not just what we had already heard, but anything else He might say tomorrow. Yes, He said many difficult things. But when He asked His disciples if they would leave him, St. Peter said, "Lord, to whom shall we go? You have the words of eternal life" (John 6:68). Indeed.

Growing in grace doesn't mean earning our way into Heaven. Rather, it's like the way we learned as children. Our mother wanted us to grow and learn and take steps on our own. First, she carried us, then she held us by the hand, and now that we can walk on our own, she is there to guide and protect us, to encourage us, to pray for us, to love us. As children, we don't earn a parent's love by what we do; rather, we grow in the way that our parents know is best for us when we learn from them and obey them. If this is true for ordinary human parents, how much more it is true for Our Lady, whom Our Lord gave us for a Mother as God is our Father!

In my memoir, *Not God's Type*, I wrote these words, just a few months after being reconciled with the Church:

What can I say about becoming Catholic?

1. It is by far the best thing I've ever done.

2. It is the most significant event of my life.

3. It will take a lifetime fully to discover what points 1 and 2 mean.

As of this writing, I have been a Catholic for a bit over four years, and those words are as true now as when I wrote them—and I say them now with even more joy and gratitude.

Chapter 3

Like the Dewfall

Mark Drogin

I was born an atheist, and my parents were born atheists. My parents and grandparents were also all Jewish — that is, they were culturally Jewish atheists. We knew that God does not exist in the way we knew the sky was blue; it was simply a fact of life. When I was a child, I did not ask — and I did not know anyone who asked — whether God exists.

I have now been Catholic for forty-three years. And yet I remain Jewish: I am Jewish *and* Catholic.

I have often been asked to tell my "conversion story." The archetypal conversion story is the story of the prodigal son who repented and returned. In the language of Jesus and His audience, the same word meant both "repent" and "return." My story describes repentance and returning to our Father.

∞

The Catholic Faith is a free and undeserved gift from God; it came to me like the dewfall — in silence and mystery — but it was not magic. Human participation is necessary. Pope Paul VI called it the "marriage of divine and human action."[4] We cannot earn or manufacture faith. Faith is a gift, and yet we must take action to cooperate with God's will.

But let's turn to how this has played out in my story. I was born into a family of not only Jewish atheists, but Jewish socialists. We had a very strong and unquestioned Jewish identity. We celebrated Passover and Hanukah even though my father believed that religion is "the opiate of the masses."

My grandparents came to the United States from Eastern Europe between 1900 and 1910 along with millions of other Jews from that part of the world. All four of my grandparents settled in the center of Los Angeles, where both my parents were born in 1915. My parents and grandparents were part of a community of Jewish socialists in Echo Park, a section of Los Angeles known as "Red Hill" because so many socialists lived there.

I was immersed in this atheistic-Jewish-socialist worldview; religion was assumed to be superstitious nonsense. At the same time, our Jewish identity was unquestioned. I had no idea what it *meant* to be Jewish, but I knew that I *was* Jewish. I realize now what a contradiction this seems to be, but when I was a child, I saw no contradiction. On Passover and Hanukah every year, we celebrated Moses and the Maccabees as well as modern freedom fighters, such as Mahatma Gandhi and Martin Luther King, who liberated oppressed people.

My personal path from Jewish atheism to proudly professing my Catholic Faith was long and difficult. My dad professed that absolute truth did not exist, and I accepted this without question. In his famous homily during Saint John Paul II's funeral in 2005,

---

[4] Paul VI, Discourse March 19, 1969, quoted in John Paul II, Apostolic Exhortation *Redemptoris Custos*, August 15, 1989, no. 30.

Cardinal Joseph Ratzinger (soon to become Pope Benedict XVI) called it the "dictatorship of relativism." He spoke of this danger throughout his pontificate, and Pope Francis has continued this warning. I was born into the dictatorship of relativism.

Voices of the 1960s

My mother and father were good, loving, generous parents. This is truly a gift of grace: "God has mercy on whom he wills" (see Rom. 9:18). My parents valued honesty, hard work, education, and self-sacrifice. I learned these natural values from birth, but something was missing—what it was, I just couldn't say.

Mathematics came easy to me; in fact, I was good at anything that involved solving equations—chemistry, physics, and so forth. I was also an atheistic materialist even though I was not aware of the label. But when I went to a science and engineering college, I flunked out. I enrolled in a public university and started smoking marijuana, and soon I was taking LSD. The popular slogan in 1966 was "Turn on, tune in, and drop out." I didn't like the popularity of the slogan, but that is what I did. Many years later I realized that I had "tuned in" to the wrong voices.

Another student invited me to go on a "trip" with him. I didn't know him very well, except that he was a cousin of one of the atheist, socialist, Jewish families we knew in Echo Park, so I felt some connection with him. He drove me into the mountains north of Los Angeles at night. We hiked up the mountain in the dark and found a place to sit. He gave me some LSD, and we sat there all night. When the sun came up in the morning, it was an incredibly joyful experience. We ate some delicious oranges and enjoyed the beautiful, sunny, Southern California day. I had never imagined anything could be so good and so beautiful.

From Atheism to Catholicism

I asked how this could be, and—without hesitation—he said, "Jesus Christ." My mind was blown. I had no idea how to process this experience. He said, quite simply, "All this joy and beauty and goodness comes from Jesus Christ." As we drove back to school, he repeated several times: "It's Jesus Christ." He gave me a Bible and told me it was all in the book. I never read the Bible he gave me, and I never saw him again. I gradually forgot about the experience, dropped out of school (again), and moved to Berkeley.

From there, I moved north to Sonoma County and into a hippie commune. When we stopped using drugs, only a handful remained. We became organic-food fanatics committed to discovering "enlightenment."

The Commune

In 1969 and 1970, we encountered many "hippie Christians" or "Jesus freaks" in Northern California, so we started looking at the Bible. I was fascinated by Isaiah 53 and the story of the Suffering Servant.

Around 1971, the whole commune discovered—or rather "decided"—that Jesus is unique and the only Son of God. It followed that the Bible must be true. We promised each other that we would stay together and be a family. I accepted Jesus as my personal Savior without really understanding what that meant.

I never lost my Jewish identity, and so it was important to me that Jesus was Jewish: He is the promised Jewish Messiah, the Suffering Servant foretold by Isaiah. But I didn't have any personal relationship with Jesus and was still unfamiliar with most of the Bible.

In 1973, we saw the *Roe v. Wade* decision reported on the news. The leader of the commune told us that everyone knew that abortion is murder and that the decision was gravely wrong. A few months later, the commune watched *A Man for All Seasons*, a movie about the life of St. Thomas More. This led us to trust the traditional (and very Catholic) Douay-Rheims translation of the Bible more than the King James Authorized Version.

In 1973, I was ignorant of the significance of these events.

Now, as charming as this all might sound, in truth the commune was a cult; everyone was pressured into unanimous agreement. The cult required everyone to make "lifelong promises" to each other, or to leave. It was a form of brainwashing. I was overwhelmed by guilt: Only God knows whether this guilt was from the Holy Spirit, or simply the peer pressure of the cult. Perhaps it was both.

The most common symbol of the Holy Spirit is fire. Often the Holy Spirit is a purging fire. A purging fire descended on the commune in 1973; I was not aware of it at the time, but I realize it now. Several members left, including me. I went back to my parents' house, then got a job in downtown Los Angeles and rented a room in my old neighborhood.

The Catholic Church

I hit rock bottom in early 1974. I was twenty-eight years old and living in Los Angeles. I held this vague notion that I was a Christian and still Jewish, but I felt totally unworthy of love or attention—even God's. I had no hope. There didn't seem to be any reason to go on living, but I was afraid of suicide, so I was stuck in this pit of guilt and despair.

I felt guilty for breaking my promises to the members of the cult. More than that: I had married one of the women in the commune, and we had children. I wanted to keep my commitment as a husband and father, but I didn't know how I could. I believed that God could and would forgive me. But I *did not* believe I could keep my promises to Him or to anyone else; that is, I did not trust myself.

One day, I was informed that the members of the commune who did not leave had all become Catholics. Intrigued, I called the chancery in Los Angeles to find out more about the Catholic Church; then I tentatively began receiving instruction from a Catholic priest.

I thought I had to be perfect before Jesus would accept me. "Be perfect as your heavenly Father is perfect" (Matt. 5:48). But I knew that was impossible. Then this priest explained to me that no one has true contrition—that is, no one is perfectly sorry for his sins. *Jesus came for sinners.* He said: "Those who are well have no need of a physician, but those who are sick.... For I came not to call the righteous, but sinners" (Matt. 9:12–13).

The priest told me that if I wanted to change, I should ask Jesus and *He will help me.* He told me that we don't have to change by ourselves: We can't do it by ourselves. Jesus will pick us up out of the pit before we think we are ready—before we are perfect. Today, I hope for that future time when I will be perfect in Christ. But I ain't there yet. Believing that I did not have to be perfect before I was baptized was the tiny, faint light at the bottom of the pit; it gave me hope.

Asking for help requires humility. I was drowning in guilt. I believed I was a failure, a Judas who had betrayed my wife and my children and my friends. I was humiliated—the Holy Spirit was slowly teaching me humility.

I wandered into the church next to the rectory where I was meeting the priest and knelt in front of a statue at whose base was a prayer to Our Mother of Perpetual Help. I began praying this prayer every day and soon had it memorized. I still include it in my daily prayers:

> O Mother of Perpetual Help, in your hands do I place my eternal salvation, to you do I entrust my soul. For if you protect me, dear Mother, I fear nothing; not from my sins, because you will obtain for me the pardon of them; nor from the devils, because you are more powerful than all hell together; not even from Jesus, my Judge Himself, because by one prayer from you, He will be appeased. But one thing I fear, that in the hour of temptation I may neglect to call on you and thus perish miserably. Obtain for me, then, the pardon of my sins, love for Jesus, final perseverance, and the grace to always have recourse to you, O Mother of Perpetual Help.

I was afraid to go to Jesus. But God gave me hope through Our Mother of Perpetual Help. This hope came to me like the dewfall: I didn't see it or hear it. I was not aware of it when it happened.

I *hoped* that Our Mother of Perpetual Help would help me. It seems that Our Mother gave me hope before faith: I began to hope for faith, and to ask for faith. I asked to be baptized, even though I knew I was not ready: I took the leap of faith. I could not have taken that leap without hope—given to me through Our Mother of Perpetual Help.

I was baptized in June 1974. I was reborn. Everything was new. I was listening to different voices—those inspired by the Holy Spirit rather than the spirit of the world. The next year

I received the Sacrament of Confirmation, and my ability to listen to the Holy Spirit gradually grew stronger. I thought I was mature, but I was really still a baby. I did not know that I still had a lot to learn.

After I was baptized, I returned to the now-Catholic hippie commune. We went to Mass regularly and prayed the Rosary. We quickly became an authentic Catholic community, but the communal spirit remained: No member was allowed to own private property until 1995, more than twenty years after we became Catholic.

Everything about Christianity was new to me. The leaders of the group frequently quoted the book of Acts: "The company of those who believed were of one heart and soul.... They had everything in common" (Acts 4:32). So that's what we did. All property was communal, and we organized ourselves by the "rule of unanimity." My grandparents had participated in socialist communal experiments in Southern California in the 1920s and 1930s. Communal living seemed natural to me — and now we had Scripture quotes too!

The hippie cult may have become a Catholic community, but the cult mentality remained for decades. The Catholic family life we promoted was undermined by our communist culture. This mentality and the day-to-day reality of communism undermined — and subtly weakened — the authority and responsibility that belongs to spouses and parents.

By accepting and professing the communal life we lived, I failed to exercise properly my spousal and parental role in our family. In many ways, I allowed the commune to be the ultimate authority and provider. In retrospect, I see that one word describes these faults: hypocrisy. In the most basic aspects of our family, I was not practicing what I preached. It is truly a miracle that our children remained Catholic after we left the commune. But I was not fully aware of this hypocrisy for many years.

"You Have to Learn Patience"

Growing in the Faith, especially as a convert, takes time. Be patient. The road is rocky, rough, and steep. As for me, after more than three decades in the Church in the commune, I lost my way. My wife and I finally left the commune and moved to Irving, Texas. We made the decision during the Great Jubilee in 2000, and we moved early in 2001. (Certainly, the grace of the Great Jubilee had flowed into our lives.) One of our children described the move as our family's "exodus." Some of our older children simply said: "It's about time."

Five years after we left the community, we still had a lot of baggage. Gradually, the old feelings of guilt came back, and I felt like a failure again; but this time it was much different. I had been married for many years, with children and grandchildren. My wife and I had seven more children after we became Catholics, and a lot of other good things happened in those thirty-two years. Many different stresses and strains increased, and suddenly I felt overwhelmed with a sense of guilt, loneliness, and anger. My doctor told me that I needed to take antidepressants.

I had a spiritual director, an old Dominican priest. Every day for months, I went to him to receive the sacrament of Confession. He kept telling me: "You have to learn patience. You have to look for the little good things. If you don't look for them, you won't see them." Every day he would say, "Tell me what little good thing happened today." I whined, complained, and argued, but he gently repeated: "You have to learn patience."

Gradually, after a year or two, he started saying, "See, you *are* learning patience." After thirty-four years in the Catholic Church I was starting to learn patience—and to learn Christian suffering. I was beginning to pick up my cross.

After about two years—very slowly—I was getting back on the right road. I was starting to notice the little good things every day. My doctor said that I didn't need the antidepressants anymore—and that the visits to the priest probably helped more than the medication. The priest, humbly, said it was both.

I still pray for patience. Appropriately, it takes time to learn patience; for me, it has taken many years. "When we cry, 'Abba! Father!' it is the Spirit himself bearing witness with our spirit that we are children of God ... *provided we suffer with him* in order that we may also be glorified with him" (Rom. 8:15–17, emphasis added). Patience means suffering: It ain't easy; it ain't supposed to be. It's the Way of the Cross.

That old Dominican priest who was my spiritual director died in 2012. He had become my best friend. I went to the nursing home to say good-bye to him when he was dying, but I couldn't say good-bye. All I could say was: "I'll see you later." I still talk to him every day, and we are still best friends. Every day he tells me: "You have to learn patience. You have to look for the little good things."

Listen to the Holy Spirit. Listen to your spouse—your best friend. Listen to your guardian angel. Pray the Guardian Angel Prayer: "Angel of God, my guardian dear, to whom God's love entrusts me here, ever this day be at my side to light, to guard, to rule and guide." When you ask your guardian angel to rule you, you are asking the Holy Spirit to rule you. We go to Jesus through Mary. Why not go to the Holy Spirit through your guardian angel?

Like the Dewfall

"I am not ashamed of the gospel.... For in it the righteousness of God is revealed through faith for faith" (Rom. 1:16–17). The gift of faith continues to come to me like the dewfall. I do not hear it. I do not see it. I am not aware of it falling on me in any tangible way, and yet it covers me and refreshes me. I ask for faith—and even the inspiration to ask is a gift from God. But a human response is required: The gift of faith is the "marriage of divine and human action." Every day I wake up and see the dew glistening in that beautiful sunrise, and I say: "Thank You, Jesus!"

Both the gift and the human response are always personal; they come to and emerge from each person in a unique way. There are many who have written about their personal faith journeys: Saul of Tarsus—who became St. Paul—St. Augustine, Thomas Merton, Walker Percy, and Roy Shoeman, to mention only a few. My personal favorite, though, is *Before the Dawn* by Eugenio Zolli, who was the chief rabbi of Rome during World War II and was baptized in the Vatican in February 1945. His Baptism was widely publicized, and so he was asked many times what "converted" him. He writes: "I feel the duty of affirming that the charity of the Gospel was the light that showed the way to my old and weary heart. It is the charity that so often shines in the history of the Church and that radiated fully in the actions of Pope Pius XII."[5]

I did not see divine providence working in my life during my struggles. Only in retrospect do I recognize the Holy Spirit coming down like the dewfall. God's time is not our time. "But do not ignore this one fact, beloved, that with the Lord one day is like a thousand years and a thousand years like one day" (2

---

[5] Eugenio Zolli, *Before the Dawn* (San Francisco: Ignatius Press, 2008), 196.

Pet. 3:8). We pray in created time, but God hears and answers our prayers outside of time.

I grew up in Los Angeles with no awareness of the full name of my city: Nuestra Senora Reina de Los Angeles, "Our Lady, Queen of the Angels"! The Franciscan missionaries who traveled with St. Junipero Serra saw great significance in the name of this pueblo, and many, many prayers are attached to this place and the people who live in it.

Are those prayers limited by created time? Were St. Junipero Serra and the other founders of Los Angeles praying for me? I left Los Angeles in 1967 with no intention or desire to return to Southern California. Nevertheless, by another apparent co-incidence I returned to Los Angeles, and it was there that I was baptized. In twenty-eight years, I traveled from the "dictatorship of relativism" to a personal relationship with Jesus Christ through Our Lady of Perpetual Help—and, it seems, Our Lady was with me as Queen of the Angels all along, as well!

∞

People ask me if I had one "aha" moment. Recently, I remembered a Good Friday Liturgy I attended in 1974. At that time, I had begun saying the prayer to Our Lady of Perpetual Help but still had not decided whether I wanted to be baptized. During my lunch hour, I went to a nearby Catholic church. I still was unfamiliar with Catholicism, and I knew nothing about Good Friday. It was a parish near downtown with an elementary school, and all the students were in the church wearing their school uniforms. I paid close attention to the entire liturgy and was fascinated by the children.

I went up and kissed the cross, and watched the children kissing the cross. To my great surprise, tears began flowing down my cheeks as I watched the children; it was then that I realized that I would become a Catholic. For the first time, I knew I wanted to be baptized.

Recently, I shared this Good Friday experience with a friend, and she immediately quoted Blaise Pascal: "The heart has its reasons, which reason does not know."[6] For the first several decades of my life, I was an atheistic materialist expecting rational answers for every question. My friend helped me to see that my heart has reasons that went beyond what my head could fully understand.

The gift of faith remains a mystery. The story here is the way I remember it decades later; it is not complete. I pray that this effort will help bring God's peace and joy to those who read it. Telling this story today, forty-three years after my Baptism, has been much more difficult than I imagined.

Every day, I take the leap of faith and stumble along the dirt road—the Way of the Cross. It ain't easy. It ain't supposed to be. But Jesus does the heavy lifting. I follow Simon of Cyrene and all the others who share the load.

---

[6] Blaise Pascal, *Pensées* 4, 277.

Chapter 4

∽

My Search for Meaning

Fr. John Bartunek, LC, SThD

We weren't hard-core atheists. We weren't dogmatic atheists, either. We were just, well, I guess the best term is practical atheists. Except for my dad, that is. He knew for sure that he didn't believe in God and that he didn't need any religion. But even he never talked about it; in fact, I didn't know he was an atheist until, as a teenager, I started to show an interest in religion and he confronted me. But that's what I mean: We never talked about God, church, religion, or anything transcendental. And so I began my conscious life expecting to find all that I desired and all that would make me happy here in this terrestrial sphere.

A "Typical" American Family

I grew up in the eastern suburbs of Cleveland, Ohio, as the middle child of three, between two sisters. My parents separated when I was five years old; then they divorced. My sisters and I lived with Mom until she was diagnosed with multiple sclerosis; then we moved in with Dad. But Dad felt that we needed a mom around, so he hooked up with a divorcee who had two kids of her own, and we moved in with them. I thought they were married, but later on Dad told me they never were—and it didn't last long anyway. I don't know all the details, but after about six months my dad pulled us out of there and found temporary housing. Soon he bought his own house, and when I was nine and a half years old, we moved into what would be our family home. At that point, Dad gave up on the idea of marriage altogether and decided to raise his three children on his own.

That winter my mom died. I remember going to the funeral, but I don't remember any conversations with anyone about where she had gone, or how sad it was that she had passed away, or whether we should pray for her. Those were religious topics, and religion just wasn't a part of our lives. It was so much *not* a part of our lives that we—or at least I—didn't even notice that it wasn't there. How can you notice the absence of something that has never been present?

A Natural Ethos

In place of religion my dad believed in hard work and honesty. He modeled both those virtues, and he inculcated them in us intentionally. My dad was also an avid athlete: He had played several years of minor-league baseball and had been an amateur boxing champion. His discipline and work ethic grew out of and fed into his love of sports. And so, natural values such as discipline, focus, integrity, respect, and achievement became the core elements of our worldview growing up under his fatherhood.

And, in truth, that ethos served me well, giving me character traits to aim for while growing up. I threw myself into schoolwork; every class was a challenge and an opportunity. Every year

I had at least one teacher who could really inspire and encourage, so my time in school became enjoyable and precious.

My family ethos likewise enabled me to see all my extracurricular activities as chances for me to grow, to be challenged, and to achieve. I became involved in organized sports as soon as they were available. I was attracted to the arts as well, and I tried out for plays even while I was in elementary school. Academics, sports, and theater effectively took up my time, energy, and attention.

This ethos also protected me from damaging influences. Drugs, drinking, and promiscuity all threatened success in the classroom, on the playing field, and on stage. And these vices all involved some kind of dishonesty or disrespect, so even without a religious element in my upbringing, the values promulgated by my dad kept me from dangerous choices. I don't remember even feeling very tempted by them while growing up.

During those years, with my dad's encouragement, I became an avid reader. This is important, because my faith journey took a particularly intellectual slant later on. I think my love for ideas and culture began in my childhood with my love for reading. Any free time I had would usually be spent with a book. My dad had given me the green light, but my mother's absence influenced this development, as well: My middle school had a yearly Read-a-Thon to benefit multiple-sclerosis research. I felt my participation was a way to show my love for my deceased mother by reading as many books as possible and getting as many sponsors as I could to help the cause. This too absorbed the energy of my mind and heart in a constructive way.

Looking back, I wonder if, without realizing it, I was experiencing the reality of the spiritual realm—the love that links us to each other even beyond the grave. Maybe even then the

Lord was planting seeds in my soul that would later bear fruit in discovering and accepting the Catholic Faith.

Religion Makes an Appearance

But you can keep religion at bay for only so long. At some point, the question of God comes up, and you have to face it one way or another. For me, it came up through the influence of my older sister. She was an extraordinarily talented and successful young woman in many areas, one of which, naturally, was sports. But when she was a teenager, her promising athletic career hit a roadblock when she blew out her knee. During the challenging and frustrating process of recuperation, a coach and some friends shared their Christian faith with her. Something about their words and testimony moved her heart, and she became a believer. She began attending a nondenominational Christian church on Sundays.

I was only in eighth grade at the time, and until then my only experience of religion had been an occasional trip to church on Sunday if I happened to spend the weekend at a churchgoing friend's house. Those trips, however, left me indifferent. I recognized that a lot of people valued church, God, and religion, but my dad didn't seem to need them, and my family didn't seem to need them, so I wasn't even curious.

But then my sister said something to change that. It was around Christmas. We celebrated a kind of secular Christmas, with trees and lights and cookies and gifts and family get-togethers, but without prayer and church. We had our lovely tree up in our living room, and Christmas Day was just around the corner. Some early Christmas presents had arrived from friends and relatives, and my dad had already placed them under the tree. My little sister and I were sitting on the floor near them, picking them up, shaking and examining them, trying to guess what they might be. My older sister was in the easy chair across the room, watching us. Suddenly we noticed that she was cry-ing — at least, that's how I remember it. We looked up at her, and she began to speak to us in a way that she never had before — a way that her own recent experiences had opened up for her.

She told us that we had no idea what Christmas was re-ally about and that we didn't even know whether Mom was in Heaven. And, by the way, we were so obsessed with the presents, she couldn't help wondering if we even cared about Christmas or Mom. She finished by challenging us to go to church with her. It was a particularly poignant challenge because our mother had died a few years earlier right around Christmas.

I can't remember whether my little sister went to church or not, but I went — my first time freely choosing to go to church on Sunday. And it became a regular feature of my week from then on — not because I converted and became a believer right away, but because I enjoyed it. Young families went to this church, with lots of kids, many of whom were my age. I received a warm welcome. The actual service was usually simple — music, some prayers, a testimony or two, and always a long sermon, delivered with gusto and eloquence.

An Encounter with God

Even though I didn't believe in God, these inspiring and attrac-tive elements of the Sunday service brought me back week after week. I began to make friends and even joined the youth choir. The more I got to know the people who congregated there, the more I felt connected to this community. I realized they were believers, and though I still didn't believe, I was coming to respect their sincere efforts to live authentic and meaningful lives in harmony with the doctrines taught by their religious leaders.

In hindsight, I guess the difference between these doctrines and my father's was their focus on where true fulfillment comes from. My family ethos led me to believe that fulfillment would come from achieving more than others — reaching academic and professional milestones, winning awards, collecting accolades, and so forth — through honest and focused effort. This church community emphasized something different entirely. Fulfillment was to come from a relationship with God that showed itself in how you treated others — in behaving toward others as you would want others to behave toward you.

Interacting with members of this church community who believed that and tried to live it made an impression on me. And one day, that seed blossomed into faith. Yes, my faith emerged organically from my contact with those believers. I became a conscious believer without even trying to, even without having to be convinced on an intellectual level.

One day, after about six months of regular attendance at that church, I was singing a concert with the youth choir. It was evening, and the setting sun illuminated the stained glass windows in the back of the building. We were standing in the front of the church, performing the finale of the concert, a song called "Let There Be Light."

As we sang, my eyes drifted up to the brilliant, glowing windows. I gazed at them, and in a moment of grace, God's presence became real to me. Up to that point, when the choir director or the pastor at the church would lead us in prayer, I would never bow my head with them. I enjoyed being with these people, but the God part didn't interest me. Until now. In that instant, inexplicably, I simply knew that the "God part" actually did matter—that God Himself was real, as real as the sunlight and the music and my own self. And not only was God real, but He was also interested in my life. It's as if He opened the eyes of my soul and with the same gesture smiled at me and invited me to walk with Him—or rather to let Him walk with me.

Later on, I discovered that such a moment of grace was often referred to as being "born again." Later still, I discovered that I had been baptized as an infant. I surmise now that my experience that night in the youth choir was the first actuation of the gift of faith that Baptism had mysteriously planted in my soul, and that this actuation had been the fruit of consistent contact with other sincere believers. It wasn't that I decided to join that church simply in order to feel more part of the group. Rather, the living testimony of those men and women who were actually striving to live their faith—and finding fulfillment from it—gave me a taste of a different level of meaning in life, and that taste quickened my spiritual life.

Entering the Catacombs

With this new dimension opening up to me, I eagerly dived into every activity I could in order to learn and to grow in understanding God and the implications of having faith in Him. An older man in the youth group agreed to disciple me, which consisted of a kind of one-on-one Bible study every week. And I also started going to a Christian Athletes Bible Study, among other faith-sharing and faith-growing activities.

But this idyllic time was soon cut short. Less than a year after the quickening of my faith, I returned from choir practice one Sunday afternoon, and my dad greeted me from his chair as I entered the living room. "Oh," he said, "here comes 'John the Baptist.'" No smile took the edge off that sarcasm. He went on to tell me, passionately and definitively, that I was thenceforward forbidden to go to church. He didn't trust those people. They were fanatics. They were going to corrupt me and brainwash me. I was no longer permitted to attend any Bible studies or Sunday schools or any other religious activity at all. Period. End of story.

I retreated to my room, stunned. I didn't understand what I was doing wrong. I didn't understand why my dad could so vehemently denounce all these people whom he had never even met. The only thing that was clear was his aversion to anything having to do with religion, and this was corrupting his genuine concern for my well-being.

I don't know why, but this first encounter with direct opposition didn't engender any doubts about my new beliefs. Perhaps the existential experience had simply been so profound that it was, for the time being, impervious to doubt. But my reaction, suffused with a faith that had already begun to put down deep roots without my even realizing it, surprised me. I remember throwing myself on my bed and wondering what I should do.

Unbidden, ideas that I had come across in the book of Proverbs, a book that I really loved and regularly dipped into, came into my head—ideas that described, over and over again, how wise sons obeyed their fathers. In fact, that sentiment is expressed at least once in almost every chapter of Proverbs. And that sentiment won out. I concluded that God wouldn't contradict Himself, so if He wanted me to obey my dad, and my dad wanted me to abandon my Christian activities—at least the external ones—then that is what I would do. I became a closet Christian, continuing to believe in Jesus and trying to follow Him in my own way, but not participating in any public Christian activities at all. Later, of course, I realized that there is and can be no such thing as a Christian Lone Ranger, but at the moment I thought I could make it work.

The "Hid Battlements of Eternity"

Without any fresh input or the support of Christian fellowship, my fervor gradually waned throughout high school. But my faith remained. The family ethos of hard work and pursuit of excellence was enough to keep me busy, and I set my sights on getting into a top-notch college, where I could go and flourish and live my faith however I wanted to. It all went according to plan, and soon I was a freshman at Stanford University. California was far away from Cleveland; all the vast resources of a great university were at my disposal; and I was now free to find a church on my own terms and to start a new chapter of my life.

Without my planning it, that chapter took on a strong intellectual bent. Having already been accepted into college, I didn't feel such a compulsive need to get involved in extracurricular activities, as I did in high school. I felt free to focus on what was drawing my heart, and that was simply *learning*.

I entered a special freshman program that allowed me to fulfill almost all the general undergraduate requirements in a single year through a residence-based, Great Works seminar called Structured Liberal Education. It was like being in a small liberal-arts college while retaining access to all that the Stanford campus had to offer. Studying the Great Works of Western civilization, even though it was through a secular lens, exposed me to what Mortimer Adler dubbed the "great conversation." We delved into, savored, and wrestled with the most gripping and enduring artistic and philosophical expressions of the human spirit—not as a mere academic exercise, but as a way of discovering our own selves. I felt as if my soul were coming to life for the first time, awaking from some kind of sleep, and I couldn't get enough of it. I still marvel at how this intellectual and existential journey—what the secular world might dub "self-discovery"—actually led me far *beyond* and *outside* myself, to encounter Jesus Christ and His sacrament of salvation, the Catholic Church.

No specific idea or thinker dominated my mind that year, but the underlying, passionate search for lasting meaning that gave unity and coherence to the great conversation resonated with the deepest reaches of my mind and heart. I eventually found a sincere group of Christian college students who helped me jump-start my faith, but the real engine of my college years became a driving thirst for that *lasting meaning.* I believed it was somehow to be found through Jesus, but I also knew that I was supposed to put my whole being into the search, just as so many Christian scholars, artists, and statesman through the centuries had done. For me, my years at the university were years of exploring and searching for the meaning of life.

At this point, my perception of the Catholic Church was tarnished by prejudice. I had uncritically imbibed what others had told me—that the Church was corrupt, that the Church had obscured true Christianity, and so forth. That all began to change one evening after a simple dinner and a discussion about Buddhism.

A Post-Atheist's Ploy

As a sophomore, I wanted to learn about all the great world religions, and so I was engaged in an independent study with a professor of history who had agreed to teach me about Buddhism. He was Jewish by ancestry and cultural background, but "post-atheist" when it came to issues of faith. As he explained it to me, this meant that he believed that the existence or nonexistence of God wasn't even a relevant question. Religion only obscured our pursuit of truth.

He and I would meet weekly to discuss readings he would give me about Buddhism, but the funny thing was that our discussions about Buddhism always seemed to become discussions about why I shouldn't be a Christian, or even a believer of any stripe at all. He was actively trying to deconvert me. I wasn't intimidated, and I actively tried to *convert him*, even though he was an accomplished intellectual and one of the most brilliant men I had met.

One of these conversations got heated. At a certain point, he said to me: "If you have to be religious — which you shouldn't be — there are only two real religions in the world. There's Judaism, and there's Roman Catholicism. And you're not Jewish!" He proceeded to criticize mercilessly the nondenominational, Protestant Christianity that I had embraced, calling it a personality cult and group therapy, not authentic religion. And then he went on to praise Roman Catholicism as a place where authentic mystery, worship, and transcendence were center stage.

I couldn't digest this. Here was an intellectually gifted post-atheist Jew and professor of history who was trying to convince me to become a Catholic! He had absolutely nothing to gain from such a ploy, and so it struck me that he must actually be sincere — that he must actually be convinced that Catholicism has something special and substantial to offer. It sparked my curiosity. Maybe I had the wrong idea of Roman Catholicism. Maybe I should look into it more.

From Atheism to Catholicism

A Renaissance Affair

And so I did.

In my junior year, I decided to spend some time studying at the university's overseas campuses in Florence and Krakow. As a budding historian (or so I considered myself), I figured I ought to experience some new cultures. Italy and Poland are two profoundly Catholic countries and cultures, and although I hadn't chosen those campuses for that reason, I consciously decided to let myself hear what they had to say about the Church while I was there.

In Florence, the cradle of the Renaissance, I fell in love with the beauty of the art and the architecture. The mysterious appeal of Renaissance art is less superficial and whimsical than the loveliness of, for example, Impressionism's aesthetic. It embodies a worldview blending faith, philosophy, science, and story. I simply couldn't get enough of it. I was mesmerized by the vibrancy of the austere hope it captured and communicated. And I was shocked to discover that this great cultural movement had arisen from and been nourished by a profoundly Catholic culture and worldview. Not only that, but the official representatives of the Church had been among its most energetic supporters and patrons.

This beauty, which captivated my mind as well as my heart, clearly held some of the secret to lasting meaning that I was searching for. My efforts to discover and to possess that secret inevitably led me to a series of encounters with believing Catholics that inspired a desire to learn more about that ancient Faith, a Faith so rich and powerful as to be able to bring into existence these works of art, these testimonies to the nobility and yearning and creative capacity of the human spirit.

Communist Fallout

But the Renaissance was in the past. When I went to Krakow in the spring of 1989, on the cusp of the fall of the Berlin Wall, I encountered the Catholic Church of the present. As we studied the recent history of the communist bloc, I found myself stumbling across the omnipresent influence of that same Church that had nurtured the accomplishments of the Renaissance. Yet we were five hundred years beyond Donatello's Florence.

The presence of the Catholic Faith showed itself not only in my studies, but also in the streets. Where there was hope for greater freedom, for greater dignity, for a fresh start, for liberation from the suffocation of communist ideology — wherever such spiritual vital signs were present, the Catholic Church was also present. The Faith, as articulated so heroically by the towering figure of the Polish Pope, St. John Paul II, was clearly the hidden fount of that vitality. Even a non-Catholic observer like me could detect it on every level — in the places where people met, in the images they revered, in the people they looked for guidance, in the way they found strength to resist the totalitarian threat, and so on. Every arm of the spiral wound its way back to an altar in a Catholic church and a tabernacle with its silent sanctuary lamp standing watch. My search led me, over and over again, to encounters with people whose Catholic Faith was changing their lives and giving direction to the most dramatic, frontline struggle for justice and truth in the world at the time.

My misinformed prejudices against the Catholic Church began to fall away, even without my addressing them directly. But more than that, my thirst for a spiritual power that could fuel lasting, vibrant *meaning* in my life — a meaning without which, I was convinced, I could never be truly happy — began to be quenched. My mind and my heart were filled with these Catholic encounters: vital, living encounters with a truth that shone with beauty and reached out to give hope to the hopeless and the persecuted. It may sound corny or exaggerated, but during that year overseas I fell in love with the Church. By year's end, though I wasn't officially Catholic, and though I didn't have all the answers to all my specific questions, I knew that I had found the Answer. Here was the meaning I yearned for, and it had already conquered my heart.

In fact, I first identified my priestly vocation even before I had been confirmed. My journey to the Catholic Church, it turned out, was also my journey to the priesthood. It wasn't one and then the other; they were one and the same.

God Calls

I remember the moment when I heard God calling me to the priesthood. It was during that spring semester in Poland; a friend and I attended Mass (purely out of cultural interest, or so we thought) at the famous Church of the Lord's Ark in Nowa Huta, an old communist factory town. When the town was founded, the communists forbade the building of churches. But the future St. John Paul II was bishop of the region at the time, and he fought hard—and ultimately successfully—to make sure that this new city would have a place of worship. The result, this Church of the Ark, became a worldwide sign of hope. Catholics all over the globe, and even Pope Paul VI himself, sent contributions to help build it.

We arrived early and went up to the balcony to have a good view. I was struck at first by the emptiness of the nave; there were no pews! But as the congregation assembled, I soon understood why: There wasn't *room* for pews, because there were so many people.

Though I didn't know anything at that time about the structure of the Mass, at the Elevation of the Host and the Chalice I could feel the spiritual force and the power of worship washing over me like a wave of grace. The Elevation was extended, and all the members of the huge congregation were on their knees in rapt, silent adoration. Even without understanding the theology, I could feel the holiness of that moment. It moved me in a way I had never been moved before.

After Mass, my friend and I shuffled out of the church in a daze. We got on the electric tram to get back to the dormitory, where my friend, an English major, wrote furiously in his journal. I stood, looking out the greasy windows at the sunlight, savoring the indescribable experience. As I stood there, halfway back to the dorm, I heard the Lord speak in my heart: "John, you should be a priest." I reacted with a smile and a chuckle, thinking that my girlfriend back in California would get a kick out of the thought. But that was the seed of my vocation, planted even before I joined the Church. It was a true invitation from God. From that moment on, the idea of being a priest never left my mind. It just kept growing, gradually and gently, like a sunrise. It accompanied my official entrance into the Church two years later, and led me to the novitiate of my order soon after that.

A Smooth Transition

For another few years after returning to the States, I filled in the gaps of my Catholic knowledge through study, prayer, and more life experience, even though in my heart I already knew that I wanted to become Catholic. I received the sacrament of Confirmation on December 27, 1991.

From Atheism to Catholicism

The journey from atheist to evangelical Christian to Catholic was a joyful journey of discovery. When I embraced that first nondenominational community, I knew that I loved Christ and believed in the power of the Sacred Scriptures to nourish my relationship with God. What I began to find as I explored Catholicism didn't negate that, but enhanced it.

I discovered that the story of my relationship with Jesus was a thread woven into a much grander story: twenty centuries of growth and expansion of the Church that Jesus Himself founded, evangelizing human culture and creating a new, wonderful civilization. God was still giving me Jesus and the Bible, but He was also offering me the sacraments, the saints, and the inexhaustible richness of multiple liturgical and artistic traditions that continued, in a sense, the very Incarnation through which Jesus had worked our redemption. Through God's grace, I gradually discovered that that amazing Story—the only Story that would reach its climax in an everlasting Kingdom—was also *my* story, and that I could play a part in it. *There* was the meaning, the lasting meaning, the full meaning, that I had been longing for.

I am still the only Catholic in my family, but I had the great joy to accompany my father during his last weeks of life, weeks in which he opened himself to God's grace and died under the Lord's mercy. And since my priestly ordination in 2003, the Lord has never ceased to give me opportunities to share with others what He so generously has given me. My main ministries have been writing and teaching, but through the priestly duties of administering the sacraments and giving spiritual direction, I find myself continuing to discover new horizons in my own journey. With Jesus, there is always more to discover, so it seems, and I am so grateful for the chance to keep discovering it.

Chapter 5

Finding God in His Creation

J. Charles Spivak, MD

*The heavens are telling the glory of God; and the firma-
ment proclaims his handiwork. Day to day pours forth speech,
and night to night declares knowledge. (Ps. 19:1–2)*

I was born in the mid-1950s to two wonderful Catholic parents,
who raised me in the Faith. Throughout my childhood and ado-
lescence I never seriously doubted God's existence. However,
when I went to college, in 1974, I began to raise that fundamental question with myself. Was I a Christian simply because I was
raised in a Christian household in a Christian country? What if I
had been raised in Saudi Arabia, India, or China—would I have
had the same faith in Islam, Hinduism, or Buddhism as I had in
Catholicism? These queries began to corrode my simple faith.

In the seventies, the universe was believed to be infinitely—or
nearly infinitely—old, and there seemed to be good scientific evidence that explained our existence without involving a Creator.
And so, by the time I graduated college, I was convinced that we
were but chance products of a universe that was itself a product of
chance. I called myself an agnostic because it seemed presumptu-
ous to call oneself an atheist, since that implied absolute certainty

that there was no God. After college I went to medical school, did my residency, passed boards, established my practice, and began raising a family. Over those two decades I gave no serious thought to the question of God.

In the early nineties I finally had time to study something not related to medicine: astronomy and cosmology, in which science was advancing rapidly. And soon I found that my comfortable agnosticism was being challenged.

On April 24, 1992, a deep-space satellite provided stunning confirmation of the hot big-bang event that began the expansion of the universe—all the matter and energy and the four dimensions of space and time—from an infinitesimally small point. Numerous discoveries since have only solidified this hypothesis, demonstrating point by point that the universe has expanded and cooled since that event. But this presented a huge problem: If the universe was created 13.799 billion years ago, then the possibility exists for a Creator! A non-God universe needs to be infinitely old for chance creation to be a reasonable explanation.

Fr. Georges Lemaître, a Belgian priest and astronomer, is known as the first person to propose the theory of the big bang in 1927. But, as I would soon come to appreciate, that honor actually goes to the author of Genesis. The first line of the Bible states: "In the beginning God created the heavens and the earth" (Gen. 1:1). A fuller translation of the Hebrew, however, would be: "At a point in the finite past the Triune God made the entire universe out of nothing." The author of the letter to the Hebrews also saw this when he said, "By faith we understand that the world was created by the word of God, so that what is seen was made out of things which do not appear" (Heb. 11:3).

In the spring of 1995, a partner of mine invited me to hear a talk by Dr. Hugh Ross at his church. Before I could politely decline, he told me that Dr. Ross was an astrophysicist from California who ran an organization called Reasons to Believe that synthesized faith and science. That was enough to pique my interest, so I went—and it changed the course of my life. For the first time, I heard solid, reasoned arguments for the existence of God. I bought and read Dr. Ross's book *The Creator and the Cosmos*, and I found that my recent study of cosmology had prepared my heart and mind to be able to understand his arguments for the Christian God.

Dr. Ross stated that God has revealed Himself through two sources—Sacred Scripture and nature. Since both have the same Author, and God cannot lie or deceive, the words of the Bible and the facts of nature *must* agree. If they appear to disagree, then either the Scripture has been misunderstood or the science is wrong. A good example of this is the apparent disagreement between the first chapter of Genesis and the discoveries of science. Young Earth Creationists understand Scripture to say that the earth was created in 6 24-hour days roughly 6,000 years ago, but science says that the earth is 4.54 billion years old. These young-earth believers base their timeline on a translation of the Hebrew word *yom* as a literal 24-hour day. But this is only one possible translation. *Yom* can also be understood to mean a 12-hour day (sunrise to sunset), a portion of the daylight hours, or a finite but extended period of time (such as, in English, "the day of the dinosaur"). If one takes *yom* to mean a finite but extended period, then Scripture and science can be brought into accord!

Over the next several months, I read dozens of books and listened to hundreds of hours of tapes about faith and science, and by the end, I felt I had more than enough evidence to accept that the Christian God did indeed exist. And then, one night in the fall of 1995, I was reading on my porch when I discerned that God was speaking to my heart, challenging me to accept Him. I had to make my choice, and I knew with certainty that, had I chosen to reject God, my heart would have been hardened like Pharaoh's, and I would have spent the rest of my life as an embittered agnostic — and I would have spent eternity separated from my Creator. Blessedly, I chose to turn my life over to God.

Here, now, are the six concepts and discoveries that most challenged my agnosticism — the six ideas that ultimately led me back to the Faith.

Problem 1: The universe is not infinitely old
We now know that the universe began nearly 14 billion years ago, so it couldn't have been the chance result of preexisting elements. This fact also opens the door to the fact that there is a Creator. More specifically, it opens the door to the biblical account of creation. The author of Genesis told us 3,300 years ago what scientists proved only in the 1990s: At some point in the past, the universe started from nothing.

These discoveries about the *beginning* of the universe were further proof of what Albert Einstein had predicted nearly a century earlier: General relativity theory showed that space *and* time had to *begin*. Einstein's general relativity theory, it turns out, is one of the best-tested and best-proven theories in science today. Further discoveries about the nature of the universe prompted the English astronomer Sir Arthur Eddington to state, in his book *The Nature of the Physical World*, that "religion first became possible for a reasonable man of science in the year 1927" — the year Edwin Hubble established that the universe was expanding. When Einstein learned of Hubble's work, he realized that his theory had correctly predicted the universe's beginning and subsequent expansion; he considered his initial doubt of the implications of his own theory to be the greatest blunder of his life.

Problem 2: The universe is finely tuned

There are many parameters that govern our universe—forces such as gravity and the qualities of atoms that keep matter together—and if these parameters are varied just slightly, life or even the universe itself could not exist! It is so finely tuned that it now appears that we are what the universe had in mind: The universe is conspicuously well organized for human existence and has all the necessary and narrowly defined characteristics to make man and his sustained survival possible. It would take a book to explain all these parameters, so I will list just a few that demonstrate the point.

If the "strong nuclear forces" that hold protons and neutrons together were 2 percent weaker, only hydrogen would exist, and nothing like the universe we know would be possible. And if they were 0.3 percent stronger, hydrogen would be rare and life would be impossible.

The neutron is 0.138 percent more massive than the proton, and at creation seven times more protons were created than neutrons. If neutrons were 0.1 percent more massive, so few neutrons would have emerged from the big bang that life would not have been possible. If neutrons were 0.1 percent less massive, the universe would have collapsed into neutron stars or black holes—and again, life would have been impossible. Nobody knows *why* neutrons are larger—except that this is necessary to allow the universe to exist and support life.

Unless the number of electrons in the universe is equivalent to the number of protons to an accuracy of one part in 10^{37} or better, electromagnetic forces would have overcome gravitational forces, and so stars and galaxies would have never formed. With that many dimes — ten to the thirty-seventh power — you could cover North America, with the dimes stacked to the moon, and do this a billion more times. If you colored one dime red and blindfolded yourself, your chance of picking it out would be 1 in 10^{37}!

The expansion rate of the universe determines what kinds of stars, if any, are able to form. If the rate of expansion were slightly less, the whole universe would have collapsed before any sun-type stars could have settled into stability. If the universe were expanding slightly more rapidly, no stars or galaxies could condense. According to the theoretical physicist Alan Guth, this expansion rate must be fine-tuned to an accuracy of one part in 10^{55}. As massive as that number is, the gravitational constant must be fine-tuned to one part in 10^{60}, and dark energy density to one part in 10^{120}. To get an idea of just how large these numbers are: The number of cells in the human body is roughly 10^{14}, and the number of seconds since time began 13.8 billion years ago is only 10^{20}!

The list of "coincidences" goes on and on. It turns out that the slightest tinkering with the fundamental forces of physics makes life and the universe as we know it impossible!

If the universe appears to be finely tuned for life, it is logical to conclude that it *could* be so organized by a transcendent God. That is, it appears to be finely tuned because it is! Atheists cannot accept the explanation of a transcendent God, so they have come up with untestable guesses, such as the idea that there are an infinite number of universes and this one just happens to be the right one for life. This requires as much or more "faith" than anything in Christian doctrine.

Problem 3: Biology's big bang

Science tells us that the earth is 4.54 billion years old and that life first appeared here 3.83 billion years ago—literally at the first moment in the earth's history that would allow its presence. The nucleated cell arrived 1.2 billion years ago, again in a sudden event.

At the beginning of the Cambrian Period, 542 million years ago—the equivalent of day 5 in the Genesis account—came biology's big bang. There was an explosion of highly organized life forms for which not a single ancestral fossil can be found. The Precambrian strata of rock is perfectly suited for the preservation of these transitional species that Darwinism predicts, but they *are not there*. In a geologic flash—two to five million years—five thousand species suddenly appeared—not single-cell organisms but highly organized animals with skeletons, shells, nervous systems, and complex eyes.

It is hard to see how Darwinian evolution—that is, gradual descent with modification—could explain this rapid appearance, in which most major categories of animals emerged. Even if one day it is discovered how such rapid evolution could have occurred, that would only demonstrate how God accomplished His creation.

What struck me as an agnostic was the fact that advanced life occurred at *the precise moment* conditions occurred on Earth that would allow for it. Paleontologists Niles Eldredge and Stephen Gould have pointed out that the fossil record shows that species remained in extended periods of stasis followed by quantum jumps in which species disappeared and were replaced suddenly by more advanced ones. The actual record of the appearance and development of life on Earth does indeed present a huge problem for the atheist and the agnostic.

Problem 4: Earth is the right planet
It turns out that planet Earth is no less a miracle than the universe. Earth is just the right distance from the sun for life to exist: If it were a little closer, the water would boil away; if it were a little farther away, all the water would freeze. And Earth's orbit must be circular rather than elliptical.

The atmosphere is permeable enough to let poisonous methane and ammonia escape, while holding on to life-sustaining and slightly larger water vapor. Meanwhile the sun's luminosity has increased 35 percent since life was first introduced on the earth, and this has been matched, step by step, with a clearing of the earth's atmosphere and a gradual decrease in the "greenhouse" effect.

I could go on and on: The Earth is in just the right place in a solar system that's in just the right spot in a galaxy that's in just the right location in the universe. The formation and location of the moon is essential to the progress and sustainability of life on Earth. Simply put, given the just-right size of the universe and the just-right amount of time it took to make life possible on our planet, either we are the most improbable of cosmic accidents or we are what the Creator of our universe had in mind!

Problem 5: Jesus was a historical figure
Jesus existed as a real historical person. Josephus, Tacitus, and the Jewish Talmud—all non-Christian sources—mention Jesus. We have more textual evidence of the life of Jesus than we do of the life of Julius Caesar!

And so we all must answer the question that Jesus proposed two thousand years ago: "Who do you say that I am?" (Matt. 16:15). C. S. Lewis summed up this question in *Mere Christianity*: Jesus cannot simply be a good moral leader. He ran around proclaiming to be the Son of God: He was either telling the truth, willfully deceiving people, or mentally ill. The problem for atheists is that after Jesus died on the Cross, He was resurrected on the third day! Many people saw and attested to the resurrected Christ and were willing to die for this fact.

Problem 6: The reality of conversion experiences
Over the last two thousand years, countless people have experience a radical change in the course of their lives after encountering Jesus. But it was the conversion of Saul of Tarsus that especially bothered me. I could never come up with a reasonable explanation for his conversion, other than that he really did encounter the resurrected Jesus on the road to Damascus (see Acts 9). Saul was a man who seemed to have it all: He was a Roman citizen through his father; he was a pious well-connected Jew; he was the best student of the best rabbi of his day; and he was esteemed because of his aggressive persecution of early Christians. But after his encounter with Christ, he found himself reviled by the Jews, distrusted by the Christians, and often beaten, stoned, and imprisoned because of his beliefs. He no longer had steady employment or income, and he had no wife or family. And it ultimately cost him his life. Why did St. Paul do what he did? There's no atheistic, materialistic account that can make sense of such a life.

My Journey Back to the Catholic Faith

By the fall of 1995, I firmly believed in the reality of the Christian God. But I didn't know which of the forty thousand denominations both suited me and expressed that truth in its fullness. On the practical side of the equation was the fact that my wife and children were Southern Baptists, and so domestic tranquility would be easiest to preserve if I were to follow suit. So, over the next three months, I read the Bible cover to cover. I now knew what the Bible said, but, much like the Ethiopian eunuch (see Acts 8:26ff.), how could I know what it meant unless someone guided me? This raised the ultimate issue of authority: Whom do I trust to guide me?

The next step was to read the early Church Fathers. I initially limited this to the writings of the first two generations of Christians—those who learned the Faith from the apostles and those who learned it from someone who knew the apostles. I figured that if the authentic Faith could not be passed through the first two generations of Christians, I probably needed to reassess and go back to square one. What became abundantly clear was that the early Church Fathers held the following beliefs:

1. The early Church was hierarchical, and the bishops were the successors of the apostles.

2. The Bishop of Rome, sitting in Peter's Chair, was the universal leader. No one questioned this leadership *per se*, just the extent of this leadership and how it interacted with that of the four other patriarchal bishops: of Constantinople, Antioch, Jerusalem, and Alexandria.

3. The Mass was a sacrifice, not just a generic celebration or commemorative meal.

4. The Eucharist was truly the Real Presence of Jesus Christ—His Body, Blood, Soul, and Divinity. No one seriously questioned this belief until after the Protestant Reformation. Even Martin Luther and Henry VIII believed this.

5. Baptism was seen as an *efficacious sign of grace*—that is, as a sacrament. The early Christians believed that Baptism actually provided remission of one's sins, initiated one into the Christian Faith, and brought one into the family of God.

6. Jesus Christ was born to a virgin.

7. The early Church called itself Catholic, from the Greek word *katholikos*, meaning "universal." The earliest recorded use of the term "Catholic Church" is the *Letter to the Smyrnaeans* that Ignatius of Antioch wrote in AD 107: "Wherever the bishop shall appear, there let the multitude also be; even as, wherever Jesus Christ is, there is the Catholic Church."

And so the question of where to place my trust and faith was quickly resolved. Only one church maintained the beliefs of the first generations of Christians: the Catholic Church.

But the problem was that the Catholic Church was simply unacceptable to me. I could not imagine making a twenty-year journey only to find myself back where I started. On the other hand, I knew that I would have to deal with the fact of the Catholic Church. Only the Catholic and certain Orthodox Churches can trace themselves directly back to the apostles. The only way to avoid returning to the Catholic Church was to prove where the Church had gone wrong. Thus began a period of intense study to disprove the Catholic Faith.

This is where my mother stepped in. She was my St. Monica, praying every day for twenty years for my return to the Faith. She called me to tell me that she had signed me up for RCIA. I had no idea what that was, so she told me that it was a class in which those interested in the Catholic Faith could learn more—and she offered to babysit our two young boys so my wife and I could attend. Because the thought of getting a weekly date night did have great appeal, we promised to go—but just to the first class.

And so, in late 1996, my wife and I showed up at RCIA, which was led by a wonderful Irish priest Fr. Mike MacMahon. Fr. Mike stressed that Catholicism is not just a "me and Jesus" religion but that we are a family—a family that meets every Sunday at Mass. Thus, in October 1996, I went alone to my first Mass in two decades. I was struck by the beauty of liturgical worship and how biblical the Mass was.

Though my journey was primarily an intellectual one, God did provide me with a number of singular graces that allowed my heart to catch up rapidly with my brain. The pieces began quickly to fall into place, and soon I found myself approaching the sacrament of Reconciliation to confess my apostasy, along with many other sins. In so doing, I was received back into the Catholic Church.

My wife and I continued to go on our weekly "dates" to the RCIA classes, but by the next Easter she had decided to remain a Baptist. Even though I was back in the Catholic Church, I had to continue to study to learn why the Church teaches what She teaches, and over time I came to understand and to believe those teachings in their fullness.

The very last issue I had to deal with, and one that I never thought I could accept, was the Church's teaching on artificial contraception. Interestingly, this was the one major point of disagreement between Catholics and Baptists where my wife sided with the Church! The teaching that most Catholics have trouble following was the one my Baptist wife always knew in her heart was right. And so we quit using contraception, and after four painful miscarriages, in our mid-forties we had our last child—a daughter who has blessed our lives beyond belief!

And remember that Protestant partner who invited me to hear the talk by Dr. Hugh Ross back in 1995? Well, he and I had numerous discussions through the years, initially about the reality of God, but later about the differences between Catholic and Protestants beliefs. And by the end of the decade, my friend had also entered the Catholic Church—proving that God does indeed have a beautiful sense of humor!

At the end of the day, there are but only two possible realities:

1. We and our universe are cosmic accidents. If this is true, then there are no absolute moral truths—only what we and our society decide to be truth. There can be no absolute right and wrong, and there is no ultimate meaning to life. This is what it means to be a materialist.

2. We and our universe are the creation of a loving Creator who wishes to have a relationship with us and ultimately to spend eternity with us. If this is true, then that Creator is the source of absolute truth, tells us right from wrong, and gives ultimate meaning to our lives.

There is great rancor between Young Earth Creationists and evolutionary atheists. But truth be told, they both suffer from the same problem: They filter everything through their philosophical preconceptions, and any data that does not fit is discarded. Atheistic evolutionists reject all evidence that leads to the possibility of a Creator, and Young Earth Creationists reject all evidence that leads to the possibility that the earth is more than a few thousand years old. *Both sides practice bad science!*

True science — the search for truth — must remain open to *all* possible answers. As St. Paul wrote to the Thessalonians: "Test everything; hold fast what is good" (1 Thess. 5:21).

Today's atheists and, sadly, some Christians are happy to set up an opposition between faith on the one hand and science and reason on the other. But the truths we discern by faith and reason all have the same author: *our Creator*! The discoveries of science don't demonstrate that "nature" works without God; they show only how God ordered nature!

Truth is truth, whether that truth is found in science or Sacred Scripture. Science can tell us *how* God has accomplished His creation, but only Scripture can provide the *why*. And both find their fullness in the Catholic Church, founded and sustained by Truth Himself.

> For what can be known about God is plain to [us], because God has shown it to [us]. Ever since the creation of the world his invisible nature, namely, his eternal power and deity, has been clearly perceived in the things that have been made. So [we] are without excuse. (see Rom. 1:19–20)

Chapter 6

∞

Called by Name

Ronda Chervin, PhD

I have called you by name, you are mine. (Isa. 43:1)

I imagine that my twin sister and I were among the most alien-ated little children in New York City. I have never met anyone with our peculiar background. We were the children, born in 1937, of unmarried parents who met in the Communist Party but had left it shortly before our birth to become informers for the FBI. (Apparently, enraged communists threatened to bomb our cradle.) Both father and mother, though militant atheists, had Jewish backgrounds, but neither had been brought up as Jews; they didn't even observe the High Holy Days at home or at a synagogue.

As right-wing political atheists of Jewish ancestry, we didn't fit in with anyone around us: not with Catholics, not with the sprinkling of Protestants, certainly not with Orthodox religious Jews in full regalia — nor Reform Jews, nor Zionist atheist Jews, nor left-wing non-Zionist Jews, and so on and so forth. Later, as a Catholic, I realized that my desire to belong to an identifiable group forever and ever had a psychological as well as a theologi-cal foundation.

From Atheism to Catholicism

My mother's parents were professional European Jews who had been invited by the czar, at the end of the nineteenth century, to help modernize Russia. Once arrived, they became fervent atheistic communists. When news reached their city that the police were rounding up suspicious revolutionaries, my grandparents, their children, and some of the Polish servants fled to the United States.

Although my grandfather, a doctor, practiced medicine among Jewish immigrants, who were mostly from Eastern Europe, the family never spoke Yiddish, that mixture of German and Hebrew that has become so associated with the Jewish diaspora. Instead, they exulted in being freethinking socialist Americans whose brotherhood was with all mankind—certainly not with ghetto Jews.

My grandfather on my father's side was of Sephardic Jew ancestry. He was born in the island nation of Curacao in the South American Caribbean and was a descendant of a Spanish family named De Sola, half of which became Catholic during the Inquisition. He was from the half that kept the Jewish faith, and he became a Madison Avenue dentist upon immigrating to the United States. My grandfather De Sola was also an atheist who never observed Jewish holidays.

My paternal grandmother was a different story altogether. She was a blond, fragile, Pennsylvania Dutch woman who met my handsome Hispanic grandfather in the dental chair. A deeply believing Christian, Grace Geist De Sola moved up the ladder socially and doctrinally from Quaker to Presbyterian to Episcopalian. She never missed church on Sundays; she prayed constantly for her atheistic husband, son, and grandchildren; and she read the Bible night and day. She was forbidden, on pain of never seeing us again, to mention God or religion to her granddaughters.

After her death, I inherited a copy of her Bible, printed in 1876, which included inked messages throughout, such as "Someday I pray that my granddaughters will read this passage."

She did insist that her son, Ralph De Sola, be baptized and attend the Presbyterian Church. But around confirmation time, my father, always brave for good or evil, stood up in the congregation and announced that he was an atheist and walked out of the church. This attitude persisted throughout my father's life. When I was growing up my parents had nothing but scorn and ridicule for my Christian grandmother. She was used as a proof of how only weak and stupid people still believe in God after Nietzsche and evolution had proven God dead or nonexistent. There's a particular cruelty in belittling elder family members.

When my sister and I were eight years old, however, our parents separated for good—and during this painful process we were sent for a few weeks to our grandmother's summer cottage on Fire Island, just off the Atlantic coast of Long Island. I felt miserable being dumped, for an indeterminate amount of time, in the house of this grandmother who loved us tenderly but whom I, channeling my parents, considered an idiot and a weakling. Seeing her opportunity to introduce us to Jesus, Grace De Sola insisted, on pain of missing dessert, that we sing this famous lullaby: "Jesus loves me, this I know, for the Bible tells me so; Jesus loves me, this I know, yes, Jesus loves me." Even though, in loyalty to our parents, we acted as if we sang that hymn only under duress, I never forgot the words.

Was that the first time I heard You, Jesus, calling my name?

Fast-forward: I was an eleven-year-old New York City girl sitting in public school at one of those old-fashioned wooden desks that had been layered with the graffiti of sixty years' worth of bored pupils. Now, once a week we had show-and-tell. Preselected students had to get up and display, say, a plastic turtle from a Christmas trip to Florida with a two-sentence narrative. It was an amusing but unassuming ritual.

But this time something different happened. There was a pause. A quiet boy none of us normally paid attention to came walking in, wearing a long black robe with a white linen blouse-like garment on top of it. He stood absolutely still, hands steepled in prayer, and started singing "Adeste Fidelis." It was the first time I had ever heard a hint of sacred music. I listened in stunned and bewildered, but joyful, silence.

Was that You, my Jesus, calling my name?

At the time, I didn't realize that this lad must have been an altar boy at the local Catholic church. My knowledge of Catholics was limited, negative, and, in hindsight, somewhat humorous. We lived in the same neighborhood that is depicted in *West Side Story*. Before the Puerto Ricans came, it was partly Jewish and partly Irish Catholic. There were only a few Catholics in the public school because most Catholic children in those days went to the Catholic school. And the only ones I recognized on the street were incipient or full-fledged members of gangs.

Why did I think they were Catholics? Because, in those days, all Catholic girls wore crucifixes around their necks, and all Catholic boys wore scapulars and sometimes had rosaries dangling out of their pockets. Besides, you could tell they were Catholics because they looked so mean.

One day I was walking home with my sister, and a group of preteen boys encircled us.

"So, what are you?"

"Are you Catholic?"

"No."

"Are you Protestant?"

"No."

"Are you Jewish?"

"No." (Our parents had never told us we had Jewish ancestry.)

"So what are you?"

"We're atheists," we answered proudly.

Having never heard of this category, they strolled off instead of beating us up as Christ-killing Jews.

Was that you, guardian angel, trying to protect us not only from physical harm but from hatred of Catholics?

How did we find out we were Jewish? Well, the public school was 99 percent Jewish, so on Jewish holidays the school was nearly empty. When we mentioned at home that we were the only ones there besides two Catholics and one Protestant, our mother reluctantly admitted, "Well, you are Jews. You can stay home." Hurrah!

Summers in New York City were and are torrid. Before air conditioning, fathers would wait until there were no policemen in sight and then use a big wrench to open the fire hydrants so that the kids on the block could cool off. It was so much fun jumping up and down in the rushing water that Jewish kids forgot their fear of the Catholic kids and jumped in, too.

Affluent Jews sent their children off to summer camp in New England or Pennsylvania. Being poor after the separation of our parents, we went to the YMCA camp. Although the YMCA was only nominally Christian, there was a tradition of having a Christmas celebration right in the middle of the July session of the camp! The leaders assembled a Nativity scene, and the Christian counselors taught all the campers how to sing carols. If the parents of Jewish children got wind of this, they were allowed to have their kids excused from the practice and the "idolatrous" ceremony of kissing the little "doll." But my sister and I were atheists, so our mother didn't mind if we learned carols. Superstitious religious stuff was garbage as doctrine, but okay as apparently meaningless custom.

Hearing "Silent Night" and "O Holy Night" sung not on the radio but live by beloved counselors, I was enchanted. It was so beautiful, somehow in a very different way from the beauty of secular classical music or popular songs.

Was that you, Mother Mary, calling me by name?

In my junior high school English class we were once given this assignment: Write a page about what you want to be when you grow up. And it had to be done on the spot. And so I wrote spontaneously: "How can I know what I want to be if I don't know the meaning of life?" I don't think I would have remembered this precocious philosophical question, a prophecy of my later choice to become a philosophy professor, had the teacher not graded it A+.

Was that You, Holy Spirit, calling me by name?

Later on I transferred from the City College of New York to the University of Rochester, mainly because I wanted to have the out-of-town collegiate experience I had read about in books. Looking for pictures for my wall, I gravitated toward a cheap print of Salvador Dali's rendering of the Crucifixion—just for its aesthetic value, or so I thought. Since I had been placed in a dorm wing of almost all New York City Jews, the other young women assumed I was a Catholic. Even though they, like me, were not very religious, they suggested I take the picture down since I was Jewish by culture even if not by faith. But I refused, without fully knowing why.

Was that You, my Jesus, calling me by name?

Like many, though not all, atheists, I was brought up to think the sexual morality of religious people was ridiculous. Out of fear of pregnancy, I had avoided going as far as sexual intercourse. But being on my own, my great wish was to shed my virginity as soon as I could find some attractive young man willing to initiate me. By God's providence I didn't get pregnant—since I would surely have had an illegal abortion if I had.

Was that You, Father of life, protecting me from lifelong guilt?

One of my companions happened to love the music of J. S. Bach. One afternoon he sat me down in the lounge and made me listen to Bach's "Wachet Auf" (Wake up), one of his most celebrated church cantatas. I didn't like choral music at all, but I sat riveted to the chair, listening with deep attention to the sacred song.

Was that you Jesus, calling me by name?

My third intimate friend was a foreign student in the philosophy graduate program. He was a German who had been in the Nazi Youth as a teen but had been saved from that terrible movement by a Catholic priest. Many of his friends became Catholic because of the ministry of this priest. He did not—but he believed that Catholicism was the only way to salvation! He hoped, so he told me, to become a Catholic someday after sowing his wild oats.

This intellectual but not actually Catholic man started feeding me the work of apologists from G. K. Chesterton to Karl Adam. Having never read the New Testament, I hardly understood a word of these treatises. But something stuck, because I started wanting to meet more Catholics even after my relationship with the German broke up.

Was that you, St. Mary Magdalene, calling me by name?

During a trip to Washington, DC, a friend and I visited the National Museum of Art, where I found Dali's *Last Supper*. I didn't like the picture at all from a purely aesthetic point of view, but I felt glued to the spot. I stared and stared at the table and at Christ, feeling mystically drawn into the picture. Fifteen minutes later, my Jewish friend had to drag me away.

Was that You, Jesus of the Eucharist, calling me by name?

Majoring in philosophy had been my way of searching for truth. But in the secular universities I attended, skepticism was so much in vogue that after a year of graduate school, I felt hopeless. Where was truth? Where was love? Why even live?

I was in this frame of mind during Thanksgiving vacation, 1958, in New York City visiting with my mother. She never watched TV during the day and never surfed channels, but for some reason on this occasion she turned on a program called *The Catholic Hour.* The guests were Dietrich von Hildebrand and his soon-to-be wife, Alice Jourdain. And they were talking about truth and love. I spontaneously wrote a letter to them in care of the television station, telling them of my unsuccessful search for truth.

It turned out that they both lived on the West Side of Manhattan—Alice two blocks from me and Dietrich ten. The letter found them, and Alice invited me for a visit. Her roommate, Madeleine (who would later marry Lyman Stebbins, founder of Catholics United for the Faith), met me at the door and ushered me into a small room. There I encountered a very European-looking woman (Alice had come from Belgium during World War II) who looked at me with such intense interest that I was immediately drawn into her heart. She suggested that I sit in on classes of Dietrich Von Hildebrand and Balduin Schwarz, his disciple, at Fordham University. Balduin's son, Stephen, then a philosophy graduate student and now a professor and pro-life apologist, could bring me up to the Bronx and show me around.

And so that's what I did. What impressed me most was not necessarily the ideas of these Catholic philosophers, which I didn't understand very well, but their personal vitality and joy. The skepticism, relativism, and historicism that characterized most secular universities at that time left many of the teachers of these doctrines and disciplines sad and desiccated. Drawn to this joy, as well as to the loving friendliness with which everyone in this circle of Catholics moved to greet a newcomer, I quickly switched to Fordham to continue my studies. That Professor Schwarz's wife was a Jewish woman who had converted from an atheistic background also made my entry into this new phase of my life easier.

After a few months at Fordham, I could not help but wonder how the brilliant lay Catholics and Jesuits in the philosophy department could believe those ideas about the existence of God, the divinity of Christ, the reality of objective truth, the absoluteness of morality, and the necessity of going to church. I could no longer believe that only stupid and weak people thought this way. What is more, they could prove in a few sentences that the mind could know truth and that there were universal ethical truths.

Was that You, Holy Spirit, removing road blocks to my eventual conversion to the Absolute Truth, which is a Trinity of Persons? Were You calling me by name?

I was sad to think that I would not be able to study with these wonderful people during the summer, when they returned to Europe. Unexpectedly, Professor Schwarz suggested that I go on a Catholic art tour with them—but I simply didn't have the money for such an adventure. When a scholarship was suddenly offered, however, I began to pack my bags for the transatlantic pilgrimage. Later I realized that this money was probably donated by one of my new acquaintances in the hope that such a trip would facilitate my conversion.

To understand the miraculous character of the events that followed, you have to know that, due to forced childhood trips to the museum with my modernist parents, I hated all art but modern art. I could go as far back as the Impressionists, whose lively and colorful pictures I enjoyed—but I couldn't bear anything earlier than the late-nineteenth century, and certainly not old-fashioned Catholic art. And, even though by now I thought that truth was real and discoverable, I had no knowledge of God, Christ, or the Church—and no interest in learning more. My only reason for going on the tour was to cling to my dear new friends.

The first miracle came when I saw Chartres Cathedral. I looked at the amazing silhouette of that church with its stunning stained-glass windows, and I started to cry. The line from Keats—"Beauty is truth, truth is beauty"—came to mind, and I asked myself, "How could this be so beautiful if there is no truth in it? How could this just be the product of medieval ignorance?"

Wasn't that You, God of Beauty, calling me by name?

The pilgrims on the Catholic art tour all went to daily Mass, and so I started going with them out of curiosity. Seeing my noble and wise philosophy professor on his knees astounded and disgusted me. I wanted to jerk him up and say no man should kneel.

Finding out that I had never read the New Testament, and seizing the moment of grace, Professor Schwarz, my godfather-to-be, searched through bookstores in Southern France until he found a Bible in English for me.

Second miracle: On the tour bus, reading the Gospels without understanding much, I fell asleep. And I had a dream. There was a large room with tables. Jesus and Mary were sitting facing me and with their backs to the wall. Mary beckoned me and said in Hebrew "Come sit with us." I don't know Hebrew, but in the dream I could understand her perfectly.

Wasn't that you, Blessed Lady of Zion, calling me by name?

Third miracle: I got the impulse to kneel on the floor of the hotel and say a skeptic's prayer that I thought my professor had told me as a joke: "God, if there is a God, save my soul, if I have a soul." The next day we went to Lourdes. My godparents-to-be, the Schwarzes, were praying that I would not be put off by the rows of trinket vendors, but I reminded them that I was "used to Forty-Second Street; nothing bothers me."

Fourth miracle: I was touched to the core by the "Immaculate Mary" hymn of the pilgrims, sung in candlelight procession in languages from around the world.

Wasn't that you, dear Immaculate Mother, calling me by name?

Fifth miracle: Once again, the art I thought I hated was used by God to reach me. In a museum in Florence I saw Da Vinci's unfinished nativity. I looked at the Virgin Mary, so simple, pure, and sweet—and again I wept. She had something I would never have: purity! For the first time I thought of myself as a sinner. I felt compelled to tell my mentors, and I was sure they would banish me. But of course, they didn't. Jesus, after all, came to save sinners.

Wasn't that you, Our Lady, who called me by name?

Sixth miracle: The face of Christ in a tapestry of Raphael "came alive," not for the others, but just for me! As you could guess, I wasn't the type to believe in such phenomena—but my mind and heart were being opened.

Wasn't that You, my Jesus, calling me by name?

Seventh miracle: The tour included a general audience with Pope Pius XII at St. Peter's. I had dreaded being bored at museums, but the idea of being in a crowd watching the Pope was more than I could stand. I decided to go shopping instead, but my mild-mannered professor insisted that I join them. So I went.

At the end of the ceremony the Pope was blessing the disabled and the sick. It was hard to see him because of the crowd, but my rather old and not terribly strong godfather-to-be lifted me up so I could see the radiant charity on the face of the Holy Father. Pope Pius XII had exactly the same expression in his eyes as the living face of Jesus in the tapestry.

Dear Holy Spirit, was that not You prompting my godfather? Was that not You, calling me by name?

Stunned by this profusion of supernatural happenings, but too much a "thinker" to proceed on that basis alone, I studied books such as Mere Christianity by C. S. Lewis. One particularly famous chapter was an intellectual turning point for me. He shows that it is incoherent to try to remain a neutral fence-sitter by claiming that Jesus was *just* a wonderful man or even prophetic philosopher. When a man claims to be divine, then either He really is God, or he is insane or a liar. There's no middle ground. And since no one thinks Jesus was insane or a liar, He must have been divine. I followed up by reading books of Chesterton and Cardinal Newman that made becoming a Catholic seem inevitable.

Wasn't that You, dear Holy Trinity, Mother Mary, guardian angel, all you saints, especially St. Edith Stein, calling me by name?

On January 4, 1959, at the age of twenty-one, I was baptized. There has never since been a moment in my life when I have regretted being a Catholic. Later my twin sister, my mother, and my husband became Catholics, making us into a hybrid Hebrew-Catholic family.

I came upon a prayer-poem of mine on the theme of being called by name. I imagine it might fit your story as well:

Tunnel of Love

Digging through
the tunnel of time,
sometimes I hear
Your song loudly,
sometimes faint,
sometimes my own
is weak,
sometimes a
full-throated cry.

When we meet,
no more signals,
deep silence,
as You carry me
into eternity.

Chapter 7

The Hell of Hatred in My Godless Heart

Joseph Pearce

Alone in a cell in London's Wormwood Scrubs prison, I stared at the twelve months of incarceration that stretched into the abysmal distance. It was two weeks before Christmas in 1985, and it was the darkest day of my life. I had been sentenced to a year's imprisonment for inciting racial hatred. I had never felt so low. So empty.

It was not the first time I had been in prison. Four years earlier, I had served a six-month sentence for the same offense, a "hate crime" under Britain's Race Relations Act. I was a leading member of a white supremacist organization who, having become involved in radical politics at the tender age of fifteen, had already spent almost ten years inciting people to hate their neighbor.

Much had happened in the four years since that first prison sentence, which is why I found myself fingering the rosary beads that someone had given me during the previous week's trial. Such beads had always been an object of my contempt. I remembered my father referring to Catholics as "bead rattlers," and I recalled the day when he had thrown my grandmother's rosary beads out the window, declaring that we would not have such "papist beads" in the house.

The anti-Catholicism that I had learned at my father's knee had been deepened and darkened by my involvement with Protestant terrorist organizations in Northern Ireland. I had traveled to Ulster on many occasions over the previous few years, during the very height of the civil war that would claim almost four thousand lives before the Good Friday peace agreement was signed in 1998. I had joined the Orange Order, an anti-Catholic secret society, and had fraternized with the leaders of terrorist groups such as the Ulster Defence Association (UDA) and the Ulster Volunteer Force (UVF). As an Orangeman I often sang an anti-Catholic song that demanded "no nuns and no priests, and no rosary beads"—and yet here I was, gently rubbing the very beads that I had always treated with such contempt.

But in that moment, I had no desire to emulate my father's example. Nothing, in fact, could be further from my thoughts or my wishes.

What I desired more than anything was simply to pray the Rosary and to enter into its mysteries. The problem, however, was the seemingly impenetrable wall of ignorance that separated me from it. I did not know the mysteries of the Rosary or even the basic prayers that the devotion comprised. Undaunted, I began to fumble the beads and mumble inarticulate prayers. It was the first time I had ever prayed, and the results were nothing short of astonishing. The eyes of faith began to open, albeit with a vision that was more misty than mystical, and a hand of healing began to caress and to soften my hardened heart. Although it would take a further three years before I would finally be received into the Catholic Church, I was taking the first faltering steps in the right direction.

Prior to this pivotal moment, it seemed that I had been going in the wrong direction my entire life. I had learned racism and anti-Catholicism nearly from birth and was taught that England was the greatest nation on earth. I realize now, as Chesterton is said to have quipped, that man does not believe in nothing when he stops believing in God: He believes in anything. In the absence of God we erect false gods and idols, such as our race or our nation.

To make matters worse, the high school I attended taught radical relativism as its own de facto religion. The school's motto —"This above all: To thine own self be true"—was taken from Shakespeare's *Hamlet*. Taught by my father to revere Shakespeare as the greatest Englishman who ever lived, I readily adopted and embraced the school's motto as my own. Throughout my life, above all else, I would be true to myself. Who could doubt such a philosophy of life? Hadn't the great Shakespeare proclaimed it himself?

I now know that Shakespeare never proclaimed any such words. He had *written* them, but he had never *said* them himself, let alone *proclaimed* them. The words are uttered by Polonius, an archrelativist and an archvillain whom Shakespeare presents in a deeply unflattering light. He serves, in fact, as Shakespeare's warning *against* the errors and dangers of relativism. Showing their ignorance of Shakespeare, the learned elders of my alma mater had chosen the words of a blithering idiot as the epitome of their educational philosophy.

Having learned the pride of ethnocentrism at home and the pride of egocentrism at school, I set out on a life that combined Nazism in politics with narcissism in morality. At the same time, I became interested in the ideas of the neo-atheist Richard Dawkins. One of the most popular books among my comrades was Dawkins's *The Selfish Gene*. I recall excited conversations in which the evolutionary biologist's ideas were used to justify racism, racial selection, and racial segregation—all of which, thanks to interpretations of Dawkins's arguments, were considered beneficial to the evolution of the species. Racism, it seemed, was in our genes and was therefore not only natural but an inexorable and positive force in the process of Darwinian evolution.

We then extrapolated Dawkins's assertion that individuals who are closely related genetically will be predisposed to act altruistically toward each other all the way to the races of man. Since people of the same race, our theory went, are more closely related genetically to each other than to members of other races, it followed from Dawkins's principles that a sense of racial kinship and loyalty was *genetically beneficial*. It also followed that racial miscegenation was biologically regressive and an affront to the progress of mankind. It was a biological "sin" against omnipotent natural selection. We then took the next argumentative step into politics: Human races and nations, being predetermined by their respective gene pools, must also seek evolutionary stability by excluding alien genes from the population.

With Dawkins as our guru, my comrades and I hailed the new "science" of sociobiology as providing irrefutable scientific justification for our racism. The idea that human behavior is determined genetically rendered moot all the outmoded Christian moral arguments against racism, freeing racists like us to frame the debate on racial questions in a new amoral light—or even to claim that racism was a positive good.

Although the organization of which I was a leading member denied that it was a neo-Nazi party, one could not graduate to the inner sanctum without tacitly accepting Nazi ideology and privately regretting the defeat of Hitler and the Third Reich.

As such, my education in racial nationalist ideology included a broad reading of essential Nazi "classics." I tried to read *Mein Kampf* with the care and reverence that the Führer's magnum opus demanded but found the experience anticlimactic. It was not that I disagreed with anything that Hitler had written; it was simply that it was a dull book. Then I read Mussolini's autobiography and was repelled by Il Duce's irrepressibly vulgar vanity — thus curing me, once and for all, of any real devotion to that particular dictator. But then I turned to the speeches of Hitler's propaganda minister, Joseph Goebbels, and found him much more appealing than his Führer. There was something utterly ruthless and uncompromising about him that was very attractive to the young racist zealot I had become.

Alongside my and my cohort's duplicitous denial of having Nazi sympathies was our denial that we were anti-Semitic. We were not anti-Semitic, we claimed, but *anti-Zionist*. Behind the scenes, however, crude anti-Semitism was rampant. Among the elite coterie of the organization, of which I was very much a part, anti-Semitism was worn as a badge of honor and seen as a de facto condition of acceptance into the inner circle of true believers. It was, therefore, almost compulsory to have read the "classics" of anti-Semitism.

I read the notorious *Protocols of the Learned Elders of Zion* but was troubled by allegations that it was a literary forgery and not the genuine minutes of a meeting of Jewish conspirators plotting world domination. Seeking reassurance, I asked one of my organization's leaders whether the *Protocols* was an authentic historical document or only an elaborate hoax. He admitted sheepishly that the document was probably a forgery but that nonetheless it retained its value as a work of prophecy of what the Jews are actually planning and doing. I was not entirely happy or comfortable with this explanation but accepted it out of a sense of duty and loyalty to the cause.

Apart from the political reading that seemed to be a compulsory part of my "education" in the ideology of what might be called "racial nationalism," I began to read literature. In so doing, I opened my eyes and my mind to an entirely new world—and a healthier one. At the time, I had no idea that my love of literature would lead me away from the darkness into which I had strayed, and into the light of a new and better way of seeing reality.

I read George Orwell's *Nineteen Eighty-Four*, which impacted me powerfully and positively. I read this classic of dystopian fiction at exactly the time that my intellect and imagination had ripened sufficiently for its fruitful reception; it dampened my enthusiasm for totalitarianism and planted the early seeds of libertarianism—or what I would now prefer to call subsidiarism—in my political consciousness. From this time on, I began to see Big Government as synonymous with Big Brother, though as a neo-Nazi I still had to accept that some form of Big Government was necessary. I was guilty of Orwellian doublethink, though I didn't realize it at the time. In the long term, such duplicity is rationally untenable, and I would eventually have to face the dilemma enunciated by the Catholic historian Lord Acton, that "power tends to corrupt and absolute power corrupts absolutely." *Nineteen Eighty-Four* pointed me in the direction of this dilemma and the clarity of the solution to it. For this reason I am indebted to George Orwell for his part in my conversion.

The one aspect of Orwell's novel that made me feel uneasy, for all its dark and penetrating power, was the ultimate pessimism suggested in the crushing of the dissident Winston Smith and the triumph of Big Brother. I desired what Tolkien would call "the consolation of the happy ending" and was uncomfortable with Orwell's portrayal of the victory of evil (yes, even as a neo-Nazi—remember that I *believed* I was on the side of what was right and good). Winston Smith's flaccid capitulation in the denouement of *Nineteen Eighty-Four* struck me as the triumph of despair.

Another work that had a beneficial influence on me was Aleksandr Solzhenitsyn's masterpiece, *The Gulag Archipelago*. I have vivid memories of sitting on the London underground with my nose in the *Gulag*, devouring volume 1 and then proceeding directly to the next. Apart from furnishing me with more reasons to oppose the communism that I already despised, it reinforced the uneasiness with Big Government that Orwell had already instilled. There was, however, one crucially important difference between the prevailing spirit in Orwell's novel and that in Solzhenitsyn's *Gulag*. Whereas Orwell's faithless pessimism permeates his work, Solzhenitsyn's indomitable faith and irrepressible spirit surmounts all the trials and tribulations about which he writes. He refused to kowtow before the god of "Progress" worshipped by the Marxists, seeing it rather as a dragon, as a manifestation of evil, as something that needed to be fought and vanquished. He did not believe in fate but in freedom—the freedom of the will and its responsibility to serve the truth. Fate was a figment of the imagination, but the dragon was real.

Furthermore, he showed that it was the duty of the good man to fight the dragon, even unto death. Solzhenitsyn fought the dragon, even though it was thousands of times bigger than he was and even though it breathed fire and had killed millions of people. He fought it because, in conscience, he could do nothing else. In doing so, he proved that faith, not fate, is the final victor. Faith can move mountains; it can move tyrannies that were thought to be gods; it can move and remove Big Brother.

From Atheism to Catholicism

Solzhenitsyn had rewritten George Orwell's novel, using as his inspiration the facts of his life rather than a cynic's pessimism. He represents the victory of Winston Smith, showing not only that truth is stranger than fiction but that it has a happier ending.

I didn't realize it at the time, but Solzhenitsyn's work and the example of his life would have a transformative influence on my own life. He would sow seeds of faith and hope in my understanding of reality and exorcise the demons of nihilism and pessimism. Something else I didn't know as I devoured Solzhenitsyn's works, and could not have believed in my wildest teenage dreams, was that I would one day meet him at his Russian home and become his biographer.

On May 28, 1982, only sixteen days after my release from my first prison sentence, Pope John Paul II became the first Roman Pontiff to visit the British Isles. As a member of the Orange Order, I opposed the Pope's visit, arguing that Britain had liberated herself from popery during the Reformation and that the Pope had no business on our islands. At the same time, however, my militant antipopery was being compromised by an emerging sympathy with some aspects of Catholicism. For instance, I rejoiced at the role that John Paul II was playing in bringing down communist tyranny. His visit to Poland in 1979 had sown the seeds for the founding of the Solidarity trade union the following year, the rise of which I supported passionately. I had also become an admirer of a number of Catholic writers and intellectuals, including G. K. Chesterton. I did not approve of their *Catholicism*—at least not at first—but I was enamored of their political and social vision.

I was originally attracted to the radical ideas of Chesterton because they represented a genuine alternative to the Big Government of the socialists and the Big Business of the multinational capitalists. Although I despised communism and its softer Siamese twin, socialism, I was also opposed to the rise of plutocratic globalism, in which organizations such as the World Bank and the International Monetary Fund used their wealth to mold global politics for their own agenda. Increasingly I perceived myself as being neither on the left nor on the right but in a distinct "third position."

My imprisonment also added momentum to my growing mistrust of Big Government, which I perceived, following Orwell, to be the crusher of freedom. Having had the weight of the modern State pressed down upon me, my love for totalitarianism had waned substantially. As such, I became less and less sympathetic toward Hitler and the legacy of the Nazi Party. I began to see, in fact, that communism and Nazism had a great deal in common. As their names indicate, National Socialism and International Socialism were united in their adherence to socialism, which might be described as the belief that Big Government is the answer to the big problems facing society. My father's biting description of a communist—someone who demands that you be his brother or he'll crack your skull—applied equally to the Nazis. I now came to see that Big Brother was essentially the same, whether he wore a swastika or a hammer and sickle. I was ready, finally and blessedly, for new ideas.

A friend suggested that I read Chesterton's *Outline of Sanity* and his essay "Reflections on a Rotten Apple." I devoured *The Outline of Sanity*, agreeing with almost everything Chesterton said and loving the way he said it. His personality, full of a vigorous *joie de vivre*, seemed to leap from the page and into the presence of the reader. More than thirty years later, I can still remember the thrill I felt when reading Chesterton's political philosophy for the first time. This passage from *The Outline of*

Sanity, evoking an idealized once and future England, resonates with me now just as it did then:

> I should maintain that there is a very large element still in England that would like a return to this simpler sort of England. Some of them understand it better than others.... But the number of people who would like to get out of the tangle of mere ramifications and communications in the town, and get back nearer to the roots of things, where things are made directly out of nature, I believe to be very large.

In Chesterton, I had found a new friend who would become the most powerful influence (besides God's grace) on my personal and intellectual development. Having read *The Outline of Sanity* I began to call myself a "distributist."

Distributism, the new creed to which I subscribed, is rooted in the principle that the possession of productive property, i.e., land and capital, is an essential guarantor of economic and political freedom. As such, a society in which many people possess such property is freer and more just than a society in which fewer people possess it. In practical terms, this means that an economy composed of many small businesses is better than an economy composed of relatively few big businesses. The same principle applied to politics means that a society composed of many small governments, such as revitalized local governments, is more just than a society composed of one big government that is separated from the needs of local people by personal, cultural, and geographic distance. Whereas capitalism concentrated the ownership of productive property into the hands of a few businessmen, socialism sought to concentrate its ownership into the hands of the State, which meant, in practical terms, handing over the ownership of property from a few businessmen to a few politicians. In both scenarios the people are deprived of the productive property that is the guarantor of their economic and political liberty. Choosing between socialism and capitalism, Chesterton wrote, "is like saying we must choose between all men going into monasteries and a few men having harems":

There is less difference than many suppose between the ideal Socialist system, in which the big businesses are run by the State, and the present Capitalist system, in which the State is run by the big businesses. They are much nearer to each other than either is to my own ideal — of breaking up the big businesses into a multitude of small businesses.

I didn't know at the time that inklings of distributism are to be found in what the Catholic Church has called *subsidiarity* and in the Church's understanding of the inviolable sanctity of the family. This connection between distributism and the family was highlighted by Chesterton:

The recognition of the family as the unit of the State is the kernel of Distributism. The insistence on ownership to protect its liberty is the shell. We that are Christians believe that the family has a divine sanction. But any reasonable pagan, if he will work it out, will discover that the family existed before the State and has prior rights; that the State exists only as a collection of families, and that its sole function is to safeguard the rights of each and all of them.

Though I was not yet a Christian I had no difficulty agreeing with Chesterton's words. I had learned to despise Big Brother in all his manifestations and was enough of a cultural traditionalist to value the role of the family in society. The idea of strengthening the family by weakening the State was deeply appealing.

The Outline of Sanity had been easy for me to read because it dealt with political and economic issues with which I could sympathize, but my reading of *The Well and the Shallows* would prove more of a challenge to my political pride and religious prejudice. I had bought the volume just for the essay "Reflections on a Rotten Apple," but I read it from cover to cover. It was one of Chesterton's last books, and much of it was a defense of his Catholic Faith. There were six separate essays at the beginning of the book, under the title "My Six Conversions," which outlined the various reasons for his embrace of Catholicism. For whatever reason, I ended up devouring these essays with the same enthusiasm with which I devoured Chesterton's political essays. I didn't necessarily agree with everything he said, but I couldn't help savoring his brilliant use of language. Even more unsettling to my own religious prejudices was the feeling that I wanted to like what Chesterton liked—even if what he liked had always been hateful to me. I have no better way of explaining this strange bond that I had formed with the man than to quote C. S. Lewis's brilliant description of Chesterton's immediate impact upon him when, as a young atheist, he had first read one of his books:

> I had never heard of him and had no idea of what he stood for; nor can I quite understand why he made such an immediate conquest of me. It might have been expected that my pessimism, my atheism, and my hatred of sentiment would have made him to me the least congenial of all authors. It would almost seem that Providence, or some

"second cause" of a very obscure kind, quite over-rules our previous tastes when It decides to bring two minds together. Liking an author may be as involuntary and improbable as falling in love. I was by now a sufficiently experienced reader to distinguish liking from agreement. I did not need to accept what Chesterton said in order to enjoy it. His humour was of the kind which I like best ... the humour which is not in any way separable from the argument but is rather (as Aristotle would say) the "bloom" on dialectic itself.... Moreover, strange as it may seem, I liked him for his goodness. I can attribute this taste to myself freely (even at that age) because it was a liking for goodness which had nothing to do with any attempt to be good myself.... It was a matter of taste: I felt the "charm" of goodness as a man feels the charm of a woman he has no intention of marrying.... In reading Chesterton ... I did not know what I was letting myself in for. A young man who wishes to remain a sound Atheist cannot be too careful of his reading.

Lewis was nineteen years old when he first read Chesterton, about the same age I was when I read *The Outline of Sanity* and *The Well and the Shallows*, and my reaction to Chesterton was exactly the same as his. It was indeed like falling in love. I had fallen in love with the wit and wisdom of Chesterton and had fallen under the charm of his humor and humility. Like Lewis, I did not know what I was letting myself in for.

I realize now what I had no way of realizing then — that it was the combination of Chesterton's eminently rational mind and his transparently virtuous heart that had captured and captivated me. It was the presence of goodness, the light of sanctity shining

forth in the darkness, the life of love that can kill all hatred. Today, more than three decades after my first reading of Chesterton,
I still give thanks to God for giving me Chesterton—and I give
thanks to Chesterton for giving me God. There can be no greater
debt than that which we have toward a friend who rescues us
from the vacuous vortex of God's absence and who leads us into
the faithful and rational majesty of His Presence.

∞

Back in that dreary London prison cell, I found myself in a state
of intellectual and spiritual confusion. I had been given the gift
of Chesterton and begun to love the rational faith that animated
his writing. And so I found myself at the beginning of twelve
months of incarceration for espousing a political creed in which
I no longer fully believed. I was at a psychological and spiritual
crossroads. It seemed that I was being asked that most pivotal of
questions: *Quo vadis?* "Where are you going?"

I didn't really know the answer, but picking up those rosary
beads and mumbling those inarticulate prayers made all the difference. The path I chose was the right one, by the grace of God,
and I knew that I needed to make a clean break and begin a new
life. Upon my release, I left London and all of my friends and comrades behind, and I moved to a quiet part of England where I could
continue to heal and to grow in the knowledge and love of Christ.

On St. Joseph's Day, 1989, at the age of twenty-eight, I was
received into the arms of Holy Mother Church. Even today,
having been saved from the wreckage of my old self, I can't help
feeling intensely the truth of the prayer we say at Mass: *Domine,
non sum dingus* ... "Lord, I am not worthy ..." And yet I am
embraced and loved by a merciful God who rejoices at the return
of His prodigal son. *Deo gratias!* Thanks be to God!

Chapter 8

∞

Paving the Road to Truth

Kevin Gerard Vost

Next, there are many who, with minds alienated from
the Faith, hate all Catholic teaching, and say that reason
alone is their teacher and guide. To heal these men of their
unbelief, and to bring them to grace and the Catholic
Faith, We think that nothing, after the supernatural help
of God, can be more useful in these days than the solid
doctrine of the Fathers and the Scholastics. (Pope Leo XIII,
Aeterni Patris: On the Restoration of Christian Philosophy)

From Catholicism to Atheism

I recently learned that in the late 1800s a group of Dominican
Sisters was called to central Illinois from their convent in Kentucky because of their remarkable ability "to educate unruly Irish
boys." I already knew from personal experience that in the 1960s
and '70s they were still very good at it, their skills extending even
to the non-Irish, and to girls as well. You see, I was the product
of Catholic grade-school education courtesy of the Springfield
Dominican Sisters and high school education courtesy of Via-
torian priests and brothers.

From Atheism to Catholicism

And yet I was a Catholic long before I met those Sisters and, in a way, even before my birth. My mother had five miscarriages before I was born, and then she was bedridden for months before my birth. This is why I carry the middle name of Gerard, after St. Gerard of Majella, the patron of expectant mothers. It was not until my forties that I discovered that one of the ancient meanings of the name Kevin, first held by St. Kevin of Glendalough, is "of fair or gentle birth"—and I don't believe my mother ever knew that!

My parents were blessed with another son and a daughter after me. We enjoyed a Catholic upbringing in that we attended Catholic schools and weekly Mass, but we did not discuss Christ at home, pray together, or read Scripture. In high school, when I had to refer to a Bible to write a paper, we drove to our local Catholic bookstore to pick one up. I was raised to revere and love God and His Church, but my faith was not really integrated into daily life. Further, perhaps because of newer catechetical methods that lacked depth and substance, I did not acquire a grasp of the fundamental truths of the Faith or knowledge of how to defend them.

Even so, in the middle of a high school religion class one day, I had an intellectual and spiritual breakthrough. The early teens are the age when psychologists say our abstract reasoning capacities first blossom, including hypothetical "if-then" thinking. Well, it occurred to me that *if* all this stuff we had been taught about Jesus was really true, *then* this is the most important stuff in the world and I should really try to live by it.

None of my Catholic friends had become similarly serious about their faith. Nonetheless, through my adolescent passion for weightlifting I had some Protestant lifting buddies at the YMCA who happily and openly declared they were "saved" and "born again." I would sometimes go with them to their nondenominational churches, where I was impressed by the sincerity, friendliness, and enthusiasm of the people; many of them were also teens or young adults, some of whom had been rescued from serious problems, such as drug abuse, through their faith in Jesus Christ. Some of the congregants would look askance when they found out I was Catholic, but I enjoyed fellowship with them and watched evangelists such as Billy Graham on television. Despite all this, I was never tempted to leave Catholicism for any other variety of Christianity. I knew full well that we also had Jesus Christ!

I spent the next few years trying to immerse myself in the things of God—but my passion for weightlifting was unwittingly leading me in a very different direction. I had become immersed in the world of bodybuilding, and in the late 1970s there was a brilliant young man by the name of Mike Mentzer—the first Mr. Universe to obtain a perfect score—who seemed to be the heir apparent to the retired Arnold Schwarzenegger. I read Mentzer's articles, attended two of his seminars, and later did telephone consultations with him and even wrote articles for a magazine he co-founded. I learned a great deal about the science of exercise and nutrition that I use to this day, but in his articles and books on bodybuilding, Mentzer also ventured into philosophy. Through his writings I encountered the great atheistic philosophers such as Friedrich Nietzsche, Bertrand Russell, and Ayn Rand.

I didn't realize at the time that St. Paul had warned us long ago to "see to it that no one makes a prey of you by philosophy and empty deceit, according to human tradition" (Col. 2:8), or that Francis Bacon wrote centuries later that "a little philosophy inclineth man's mind to atheism,"[7] for I had unwittingly offered

---

[7] Francis Bacon, "Of Atheism," in *Essays, Civil and Moral.*

my soul up as prey, and my mind did indeed inclineth that way! As Mentzer's writings shone like a beacon of truth in the foggy world of strength training, which was and is so full of conflicting training systems and hucksterism, so too did I come to believe that his beacon of truth brought the unthinking errors of religion to light.

The philosophers I was drawn to were indeed brilliant in their own fields of philology (Nietzsche), mathematics (Russell), and literature (Rand), and I assumed that brilliance would apply when they directed their minds to religion and theology. Further, these philosophers and their followers promoted the idea that intelligence should correlate with agreement with them—and with turning away from God. To someone who thinks himself quite clever, as I did, this has an undeniable appeal. Similarly, these thinkers all held that an intelligent person should put his trust in *reason*, leaving *faith* to those who lack the capacity or the will to use their minds fruitfully. A modern group of atheists capitalizing on this idea calls itself the "Brights," suggesting that believers, by contrast, must be dim.

Under the influence of my bodybuilding mentor and these classic writers, I abandoned my faith in God in my late teens.

Twenty-Five Years in the Atheistic Wilderness

Popular atheism was not as militant and contemptuous in the 1970s—in part because it wasn't as popular. I never felt compelled to speak out against the Church; having been raised in the Church, I knew there was so much good there. I respected, for example, the Church's seriousness about education and Her ethic of universal love. Indeed, as I look back, I sometimes joke that I knew the Church had so much truth and goodness, but I thought it was wrong about one little thing: the existence of God! Being pulled from Christ and His Church by philosophy—the "love of wisdom"—I believed I was pursuing the truth, and I regretted that I could no longer believe that what I had been taught was true. The first half of my original "if-then" had been removed, so the second half—the very meaning of my life until that point—had to go as well. Still, throughout my years of athe-ism, I wished that I could be convinced that I was wrong.

During my twenties and thirties, I pursued a career in disabil-ity evaluation and got married in the Catholic Church, mostly to please my Irish Catholic mother. My wife, Kathy, was a con-vert to Catholicism, and we raised our two sons in the Church and sent them to Catholic schools. I thought at the time that I preferred the "indoctrination" the children would get from the Church to the one they would get from the government. Further, I never proselytized for atheism because I knew many people received succor and courage from their faith. I thought I'd let my sons decide for themselves what they believed, once they reached adulthood. I even went to Mass at times, but I just went through the motions. In the 1990s, I also pursued master's and doctoral degrees in psychology that would later factor into my journey home to the Faith in surprising ways.

Two incidents began to move me back in the right direction. The first was in 1992. Kathy was pregnant for the fourth time. Because she had had two miscarriages after the birth of our first son, her doctor recommended that she undergo an amniocentesis procedure that included a very high-quality ultrasound. When I left the Church, I also accepted the pro-abortion position, largely on the premise that the issue pitted the rights of an *actual* per-son (the mother) against those of a *potential* person (the fetus). I recognized that position as a fraud as soon as the first images of our second son showed up on the screen. Clearly this fetus was no mere *potential* person, but an *actual* human baby. Kathy and I even thought that he looked like his brother! Based on the evidence of my senses, my return to the Church's pro-life teaching came in an instant—a full twelve years before my full return to Christ and His Church.

Five years later, I experienced another important, but far less pleasant experience. Forgetting the scriptural lesson from my childhood that "pride goes before destruction, and a haughty spirit before a fall" (Prov. 16:18), in 1997, as soon as I had obtained my doctorate in clinical psychology I jumped at the very first job offer I received—even though it was in a subspecialty in which I had no clinical background and required relocating my family to another city for the first time in our lives. I had never really failed at anything, and so I threw caution to the wind. The result of this upheaval was the first and only depressive episode in my life. Since my mid-teens I had never gone even two weeks without exercising; in that dark year, I went almost a full six months without a workout!

Depression can be so very painful, even for those of strong faith, and I found it especially debilitating without the hope that comes only from Christ. I recall at one point telling my wife how much I missed "those Christians" at my old office. Though I did not share their beliefs, these Protestant and Catholic friends, with their confidence in their faith, their willingness to share it, and their genuine Christian kindness, provided real solace when I thought about the life I had left behind.

Though I didn't know it was He at the time, God put things right again. I was able to hit the reset button on my life: I accepted a voluntary demotion to my old job; my wife was able to return to her job; our sons returned to their school; and we were able to find a new house in our old city in record time. I was even able to return to my part-time work teaching psychology at the University of Illinois at Springfield. One night, when I was teaching about psychological theories of moral development, an adult student who was going through a diaconate program gave me some Catholic materials on the virtues. I would never have believed I'd be writing about them myself within the space of a few years!

From the Wisdom of the World to the Wisdom from Above

Earlier I mentioned Francis Bacon's quip that "a little philosophy inclineth man's mind to atheism." Well, that was only the first half; here's the second: "but depth in philosophy bringeth men's mind about to religion."

By forty-three years of age I had worked pretty hard all of my adult life. I had been employed full-time in the disability field since 1984 and had returned to school to complete my master's in 1990. When I started my doctoral program in 1992, our second son was two months old. I worked full-time all through school except for the internship/dissertation year of 1997, but even that year I continued to teach one or two college courses during the evenings. After graduation I continued to work full-time and to teach college students every fall and spring term.

In the summer of 2004, however, I was struck by a phrase in the Stoic philosopher Seneca's essay on the shortness of life: *Nihil minus est hominis occupati quam vivere* (There is nothing the busy man is less busied with than living). He was talking about me! I had been so busy with busyness that I had little time to spare for the important things in life — or even for reflecting on the question of what things in life were the most important. A few months later, I would come across once more Christ's own words to His friend Martha: "You are anxious and troubled about many things; one thing is needful" (Luke 10:41–42). And so I decided to quit my part-time job, which allowed me, for the first time in years, to indulge in the pleasures of philosophy—with the most surprising results.

It was the wrong kind of philosophy that led me away from the Faith, though the people I had read were quite intelligent and had kernels of truth in some of their writings. I was influenced most of all in my atheistic years by one atheistic psychologist—Albert Ellis—and one atheistic philosopher—Ayn Rand. Both of these thinkers, it turned out, rooted their philosophy in ancient ideas. Ellis, the founder of Rational-Emotive Behavior Therapy, openly credited the Stoic philosophers, most notably Epictetus, with providing the foundation for his system of therapy. Epictetus wrote that "people are disturbed not by things, but by the views they take of things"; the idea that if we train ourselves to think about our lives more rationally and accurately, we will be able to reduce unnecessary emotional distress has become a cornerstone of modern cognitive psychotherapy. Ayn Rand, on the other hand, described her system as an outgrowth of the philosophy of Aristotle. I soon learned, however, that while Ellis and Rand were vocal atheists, the Stoics and Aristotle had argued that the use of our reason must lead us *to something*—namely, the existence of God!

It was during these months in 2004 that I began to study those ancient primary sources, and what revelations did I find there! I had enjoyed an audiotape course on *The Ethics of Aristotle* that was presented by a Catholic priest, Fr. Joseph Koterksi, SJ, and so I then purchased his DVD course on the natural law. Thus began, to my great surprise, my journey home to the doors of the Church. In the natural law course I found my great favorites, such as Aristotle and the Stoics, but then we moved along to the likes of St. Augustine and St. Thomas Aquinas. I was transfixed by the beauty and the humaneness of their teaching—and how they seemed to put the raw materials of ancient teaching to much more elegant use than my atheist mentors. Where were the great atheistic definers and defenders of the inviolable nature and inalienable rights of humankind?

It was through Fr. Koterski's recommended reading that I found myself immersed again in the writings of the psychologist and philosopher Mortimer J. Adler. Adler was raised in a nominally Jewish home and throughout most of his life delighted in declaring himself a "pagan." But he also described himself as a Thomist—a student of the philosophy of St. Thomas Aquinas. I didn't know it at the time, but Adler was eventually unable to resist the Angelic Doctor (as St. Thomas is known): In his seventies, he made the leap of faith to the Episcopalian Church, and a few years later he went all the way home to the Catholic Church.

Two of Adler's books that moved me most were *The Difference of Man and the Difference It Makes* and *How to Think about God*. Even more important, though, were the person and the writings Adler led me toward. Charles Darwin said that "[the naturalists Carl] Linnaeus and [Georges] Cuvier have been my two gods—but they were mere schoolboys compared to old Aristotle." Well, when I first read St. Thomas Aquinas it soon dawned on me that the atheistic philosophers I had been reading were mere schoolboys compared with old St. Thomas Aquinas! The Angelic Doctor authoritatively interpreted Aristotle and incorporated some of the insights of the Stoics, especially Seneca, into his *Summa Theologica*. He even reconciled apparently contradictory positions of Aristotle and Seneca. Here I found more beauty, more humanity, and more *reason* than in the atheism of Ellis or Rand or Russell.

And yet I found so much more in St. Thomas than a knowledge of and reverence for some of history's greatest teachers of worldly wisdom. In the second part of his *Summa Theologica*, Thomas examines human nature—how we think, how we feel, and how we can become happy on earth only through acquiring the virtues that perfect our human powers. As a psychologist myself, I was floored to discover that St. Thomas knew human nature far more completely than the most vaunted modern psychologists. And indeed, I recalled that even in my specialty area of memory and memory improvement, St. Thomas had made substantial contributions.[8]

It was, however, when I studied the part of the great *Summa* that addresses the existence and attributes of God that I found that all the arguments that had led me away from God in my teens had been answered most masterfully by St. Thomas more than seven hundred years ago. And indeed, as was always characteristic of him, he did so by drawing on arguments from pagan philosophers and Church Fathers who preceded him. The answers were there all these years within the treasury of our Catholic Tradition, but I didn't have a clue!

Thomas starts from raw facts available to our senses, such as the fact that things move or change or that there are causes and effects, and shows that God not only *must* exist (something or someone has to *start* the process of causing and changing) but that He must be *uncaused* and *unchangeable*. Therefore, God is not bound by time, as we are; rather He exists in *eternity*. It makes

---

[8] See St. Thomas Aquinas, *Summa Theologica*, II-II, Q. 49, art. 1, "Whether Memory Is a Part of Prudence."

no sense to talk of God doing something different tomorrow from what He plans today since God's perspective is not limited by time; all things are present to Him always. Further, Thomas shows that God can and must exist as the ground of all being. Look all around the universe, and you will find nothing that has endured forever as it is and nothing that gave itself its own existence. Matter itself just can't do that. There must be some other *necessary being* that brings into existence and sustains all merely *possible beings*, and that being is God.

These arguments are but the tip of the one-and-a-half-million-word iceberg of the *Summa Theologica* that sent my atheism plunging to the bottom of the sea. Thomas provides these "ways" to prove the existence of God that he elaborates further elsewhere, and he also writes extensively and amazingly on the attributes of God accessible to human reason. I was shocked at the shallowness of all the arguments against God that I had assumed were so ironclad. I found myself again not an atheist but *a theist!* (What a difference one little space makes!)

Still, one must make a leap of faith from the god that reason shows us—"the god of the philosophers"—to the God of Abraham, Isaac, and Jacob. Even here, though, Thomas makes the transition almost inevitable. He always proceeds from the evidence of our senses to God's existence, and then to a fuller knowledge and love of Him. This process isn't just logical; it is confirmed in sacred Scripture. In the book of Wisdom we read: "For from the greatness and beauty of created things comes a corresponding perception of the Creator" (13:5). And in the letter to the Romans St. Paul says of God: "Ever since the creation of the world his invisible nature, namely, his eternal power and deity has been clearly perceived in the things that have been made" (1:20). Clearly, the Church that Christ gave us recognizes the value of human reason in leading us *toward* the God of the Bible, whom we *join with* by that leap of faith.

Finally Home

So it happened to me just as Pope Leo XIII said it would in *Aeterni Patris*, quoted at the beginning of this chapter. I was a person committed to reason alone, and God drew me home to Himself and His Church through the writings of the Scholastic philosopher and theologian St. Thomas Aquinas, who so loved the Church Fathers that he was said to have inherited the intellects of them all. Pope Leo wrote that "philosophy, if rightly made use of by the wise, in a certain way tends to smooth and fortify the road to true faith, and to prepare the souls of its disciples for the fit reception of revelation" (*Aeterni Patris*).

I had come to see that faith and reason were not at all opposed, but were, as St. Pope John Paul II would write, the two wings on which we rise to the truth.[9] Faith does not contradict reason, but perfects it. It takes us, through the gift of God's revelation, to realities that exceed reason alone—such as the fact that the one God is three Persons, and that the second Person, the Son and the Word, took on flesh in human time so that we might share in eternal joy with Him. It was philosophy, that "love of wisdom," as taught by a man who knew that Christ was Wisdom Incarnate, that led me back home.

Reading St. Thomas also rekindled my love and understanding for the Bible, as he deftly showed not only the reasonableness of its words but also their divine beauty and goodness. In those

---

[9] St. John Paul II, Encyclical Letter *Fides et Ratio*, September 14, 1998.

early days home in the Church, it was with great delight that I read the words of Jesus Christ in the Gospels for the first time in twenty-five years. I was also filled with joy that I could rejoin the Church with my family, embrace the sacraments, and enjoy again the graces that God had there for me, available for the asking for all those years.

I will never cease thanking God for the stirrings of the Holy Spirit that led me to St. Thomas Aquinas—the man who showed me that one need not give up his reason to embrace the Catholic Faith. I've been graced to embrace in some small measure the truth that he declared: "For when a man's will is ready to believe, he loves the truth he believes, he thinks out and takes to heart whatever reasons he can find in support thereof: and in this way human reason does not exclude the merit of faith but is a sign of great merit."[10] I found, too, that in my years in the atheistic wilderness God had been quietly preparing me through my studies in psychology and philosophy to be able to share some small taste of the wisdom of St. Thomas Aquinas with contemporary Catholic audiences.

Throughout the process of returning to the Church, I learned some simple but profoundly important lessons that should give hope to anyone with friends or family members who have fallen away. First, with God there is always hope; we never know how long it might take for a person's heart and mind to open to Him. Second, never underestimate the power of prayer. When I came back to Christ, I learned from my family that they had been praying for me for years. Third, simple Christian witness and kindness can be incredibly powerful. The simplest words and acts from my

[10] St. Thomas Aquinas, *Summa Theologica*, I-II, Q. 1, art. 10.

Christian coworkers (and even my Catholic barber!) helped me along my own journey.

Lastly, I wish that every parishioner in every parish would be encouraged to discover and relish the kinds of Catholic media — modern and traditional, popular and intellectual — that are there just waiting to share the limitless truth, beauty, and goodness of Christ and His Church. To journey back home to Catholicism truly is to rejoin, to rejoice, and to reason with the most glorious family on earth — and in Heaven!

Chapter 9

∞

Christ's Willing Captive

Scott McDermott

It started with lust. My disciples gathered around me as I solemnly shared the filth of my father's pornography collection. We were ten or eleven years old and our parents at work as we took turns reading from the pages in an antiphonal liturgy of human degradation.

This was in Evansville, Indiana, where my friends were all girls, and all Catholics. My family was not Catholic; my father had no religion but lust, and my mother had fallen away. She has now come back to the Church after forty-seven years, while my father was received on his deathbed in 2012.

They took me out of Evansville when I was about to turn eleven. We moved to Mayfield, in our original home of Western Kentucky. It may be that God removed me from my circle of friends in order to stop me from poisoning the well of their purity any further.

At the time, though, I was devastated. I cried often but found no sympathy, so I turned to my drug—lust, my secret friend, which was always available and which manifested itself in habitual self-abuse. But because it is important to the story of my atheism, I must mention that my obsessions took a new and unexpected turn. Mayfield worshipped two gods: the peculiar Jesus of fundamentalism and the idol of athletics, personified by the young male athletes who year after year brought a nimbus of glory to our crumbling side streets. This is how I perceived it, anyway, as I shut myself off to the genuine goodness present in that place, as I had already done within my family. I knew and believed there could be no place for me in this new and strange homeland.

One day we were in J. C. Penney, and I saw one of my classmates standing in front of a three-way mirror. His name was Davis, and he was one of the star athletes in seventh grade. At his mother's bidding he nonchalantly shucked off his shirt, revealing a still slightly pudgy, hairless, but tan chest. I looked and wondered. It is the first time I remember the intoxication of attraction for another actual person, and henceforward this attraction would be directed toward men. It didn't take long until every male I saw anywhere became the object of my flattering attention and unceasing idolatry.

But this didn't bring me fulfillment. To the contrary, I hated myself. I felt deeply that I was inferior, as a man, to the good old boys who surrounded me. But, strange to say, I was also the *object* of much idolatry—first of all, from within my family. I said that lust was my father's religion, but that's not quite complete: Both he and my mother partook of another cult—the religion of Scott, their imperious little god, whom they loved to distraction. This was, paradoxically, part of my problem, even though I couldn't recognize it then.

The Cult of Scott spread in 1981, when I managed to win the state spelling bee and go to the National Spelling Bee in Washington, D.C. I cried when I finished 107th, but the photograph of our family on the steps of the U.S. Capitol with our congressman made the front page of the *Mayfield Messenger*. At the school assembly held in my honor, I watched, uncomprehending, as Davis applauded wildly like the young gentleman he was, a big grin on his face. It never occurred to me that one of the males I idolized might genuinely find something to admire in me.

I still hated myself—and I hated Davis, too, whose gift I could not receive—but I had found my way to power, even if I did not perceive it to be a masculine power because I always associated my intellectual strengths with my mother's teaching. Yet it was still a power—something I could use to build a public façade to conceal my decaying spirit within. I entered every academic competition, bringing home accolades like the athletes I emulated from afar. In the eyes of my hometown, I was developing into something of a local star.

But even this conditional acceptance proved to be too much love for me, and so I sought to undermine it by placing myself in opposition to the town's prevailing Christian worldview. At this time, Carl Sagan's series *Cosmos* was broadcast on PBS. It celebrated the great scientific minds of the past who, so we were told, had dispelled the shadows of medieval ignorance and taught us that our world, and indeed our entire lives, were made solely of matter. A group of fundamentalists took out an ad in the *Paducah Sun* challenging Sagan to emerge from his fastness at Cornell University, to come to Western Kentucky, and to debate evolution with them. (He declined.) So I took up the cause of my absent hero and proclaimed myself an evolutionist, then a freethinker, and an agnostic. Pressed further, I told Tammy, one of my classmates, that I was a Deist. "Oh god," she said with sincere despair, "you worship the Devil?" No, but in truth I did not worship the watchmaker-god either, so I took the final step and announced I was an atheist.

From Atheism to Catholicism

That is how I became the village atheist at age twelve. This had the effect, of course, at some level intended, of making people even more interested in me. I received a letter begging me to "believe, Scott, before it is too late," signed "A concerned Christain [sic]." A woman with a strange glow in her eyes approached me in a store to say, "Jesus loves you. You know that, don't you?" (I didn't.) Eventually I was given up as a lost cause, and attention began to be focused on my younger sister; one Sunday a family showed up on our doorstep with cookies, trying to entice her to church. All this only solidified my opposition to what I perceived to be Christian anti-intellectual tyranny that existed, it seemed to me, to stifle my burgeoning genius.

But, in truth, I had received a very good intellectual formation in Mayfield from excellent teachers, beginning with my mother, who did not see athletics as the most important thing in life. I also had a very intelligent group of friends, most of whom I met through our robust community theatrical group. One, a young man named Chip, I fell in love with. Sex was out of the question, but I longed to make him my best friend. When he finally submitted to this, I quickly lost interest, but before that occurred, he introduced me to the works of Ayn Rand.

Never having read philosophy, I was overwhelmed by the profundity of her turgid melodramas, spiced with little slogans from Aristotle such as "A is A" or "non-contradiction." (How the Philosopher would have laughed at the use she made of them!) Rand aspired to "objectivism," a system of absolute truth without God, and her worship of masculine power dovetailed nicely with my own covert religion of lust. Thanks to her, I became a full-fledged dogmatic atheist.

Even so, in public I prided myself on my scrupulous morality. Obviously I did not date girls, and aside from two furtive sexual encounters with my friend Todd, who died of AIDS at age twenty-nine, I had no sex with men either. Apart from a couple of lapses, I didn't drink, either, or even go to parties. "It's such a waste," one of my friends told me, "you'd be such a good Christian!" Like the apostate emperor Julian, I projected an image of pristine morality as inwardly I served my pagan gods of lust. This enabled me, in my monstrous intellectual pride and thoroughgoing denial, to look down on the "hypocrites" who sought to convert me.

∞

It is rare to meet a real materialist atheist these days. They are rare birds, on the evolutionary path to extinction, and I am always excited to encounter one. The current intellectual climate doubts all truth, and of course the real atheist does believe in truth — the truth that our world is a collection of particles and nothing more. This is an assertion just as dogmatic as anything the Church proposes, one that is easily picked apart by those who deny the validity of any truth claims. Agnosticism or indifferentism is far more fashionable nowadays. I was never really agnostic; even then I had a faith in objective truth that places me in kinship, even now, more with Ayn Rand or the celebrated "New Atheist" Richard Dawkins than with the denizens of our skeptical and bewildered culture.

One can attempt to show the materialist atheist that there can be no motion without a Mover or no design without a Designer, but I prefer a different approach — that of Hamlet when he says, "There are more things in heaven and on earth than are dreamt of in your philosophy, Horatio." Science can make pronouncements about matter with competence, but it cannot account for many aspects of life that we experience daily: our sense of beauty, our longing for friendship and love, our ethical intuitions, and perhaps above all, our evil and our sin. A purely material world could never have produced Seneca, Rembrandt, Mendelssohn, or St. Teresa of Calcutta, but it also could never have given birth to Hitler, Pol Pot, or Leopold and Loeb—those adolescent gay lovers who in 1924, believing themselves Nietzschean supermen, beat fourteen-year-old Bobby Franks to death with a chisel and then, on the way to dump his body in a cistern, stopped for hot dogs and root beer. If the world of the materialists lacks the composed refinement of the works of Keats or Degas, it also lacks the ingenuity to foster such studied cruelty; some malevolent intelligence that transcends mere matter must be at work.

With the garden-variety agnostic of today I would take a different tack. The typical nonbeliever is actually a post-Christian humanist who accepts many of the moral precepts of the Catholic tradition, including the transcendent dignity of human life and the fundamental value of free will. In practice, of course, he exempts certain human beings—the unborn and, increasingly, the old and the sick—from protection within his morality, but this takes place only through an intellectual sleight of hand that denies they are persons to whom we owe any duties at all. His free will, similarly, is the ever-expanding license to do almost anything imaginable, up to and including mutilating himself and pumping himself full of female hormones based on the fantasy that he can become a woman. Yet the modern secularist agnostic cherishes his freedom as passionately as we Christians do; his ideological malignancy is rooted in the terrain of a Christian anthropology. The Western world inherited by the secularist, whether he wants to admit it or not, was made and remains haunted by Christ and His Church.

To this person I would quote chapter and verse from Nietzsche, who proved unanswerably that it is impossible to get rid of the Christian God and retain any shred of Christian morality. Or, as the twentieth-century religious seeker Simone Weil observed in *Waiting for God*, if the man standing before me is but a collection of atoms, then I could easily gouge out his eyes. I would challenge the secularist agnostic, then, that he is surely uncomfortable with and likely incapable of such violence, and thus he holds some intuitions about the value of the human person. I would invite him to see that, far from being a nonbeliever, he more than likely adores many gods: perhaps environmentalism, pornography, the media, party politics, racial politics, sexual politics, or just himself.

Thus it was for me. After having been a materialist atheist in high school, I became this type of humanist agnostic when I matriculated at Cornell (where I never met Sagan, though I did make a pilgrimage to look at his strange bunker-like home, embedded in the edge of a cliff overlooking one of Ithaca's deep and beautiful chasms). I believed in human liberation and endless progress, which flies in the face of the overwhelming evidence of the twentieth century: the gulags, the Holocaust, the Bomb.

My undergraduate years were busy and formative. I got myself arrested three times, protesting apartheid in South Africa. I studied Marxism and deconstruction, though I did not study them very hard, being too busy cultivating a new persona as a romantic revolutionary on the cultural barricades. But, above all, I devoted myself to emerging from the closet and becoming a militant gay activist. This was a great step toward honesty, because even though it meant building up a new façade and conforming to the fashions and requirements of gay culture, I could now bring my lust-god out of its private sanctuary and worship it openly. I no longer called myself an atheist because I could now acknowledge my belief in something transcendent: my ideal friend, my fantasy of a perfect male lover.

I should say that during my seven-odd years as a full participant in the gay community, few of us wanted gay marriage. This came later, primarily as an effective public relations strategy on the part of gay leaders. We called our straight friends "breeders" and thought of ourselves as sexual revolutionaries. Nevertheless, all the gay men I knew cherished this fantasy of love in some form or another, even when we were having sex with men whose names we did not know.

You must understand that the pursuit of love feels entirely different for gay men than it does for the rest of humanity. From what I have observed, a typical man or woman pursues a mate somewhat like a bird watcher. He or she watches one specimen intently and then shyly approaches. A gay man acts more like a big-game hunter. Every male of the species is a potential target; he is always on the prowl, and, inevitably, if he succeeds in bringing down his quarry, he must leave it as carrion and go in search of new prey. Thus, the entire world becomes eroticized and there is no respite from the chase.

I wish every well-intentioned person who supports gay marriage because "they only want love, just as we do" could spend one minute inside the mind of a gay man. He would instantly know he had entered an entirely different state of being. I am aware that some heterosexuals are sex addicts. But it came as a revelation to me, after my conversion, that this kind of addictive and predatory behavior is not the norm—that there are people in the world who do not experience everyone of a certain gender as potential sexual conquests, and the other half of humanity as an irrelevant nuisance.

Yet I did call it love, and it did lead me to Love, albeit by a roundabout path.

One night in my junior year, the abyss opened beneath me. As so often happened, I was pulling an all-nighter, this time reading "The Bear," William Faulkner's story of a young hunter trying to bring down a great black bear. As a tentative morning glow filtered through beveled glass, I had my first panic attack. A week later, I left school for a long leave of absence. I got into therapy and eventually was able to leave the house again without fear of another debilitating panic attack. And as, for the first time, I came face-to-face with myself, I began to notice something. In its massive disorder, my life pointed to the existence of a pattern. I looked at my parents' lives, my life, my friends' lives — all had shattered against an invisible force field, a taut reality that was stronger than we were. It had broken me, but it was true, and I had to know what it was.

So I looked. At first it was a purely intellectual quest. In my classes, I frequently defended the idea of absolute truth without knowing what that truth was. Then, in the summer of 1991, I found myself alone; most of my friends were away from Ithaca. And, without knowing why, I turned to the Catholic authors I had always loved — especially Flannery O'Connor and Evelyn Waugh, whose *Brideshead Revisited* had long been my favorite novel. It began to dawn on me that perhaps Catholicism contained the truth I had been seeking. When I picked up Thomas Merton's *Seven Storey Mountain*, that impression coalesced into conviction.

But I couldn't be Catholic, could I? So I started attending the local Episcopal church, only to find the same people and the same attitudes — the relativism, the addiction to ideology — that I rebelled against at Cornell. Furtively, I stole into the tiny shop next to Ithaca's Catholic parish, Immaculate Conception, and purchased a rosary. This was the real beginning of my spiritual awakening; it was through the Blessed Mother that my soul started to open up.

Soon I felt ready to enter the confines of the church building. But the first time I walked in, I experienced a sensation of profound discomfort and shame. This came from within, of course, and not from the tabernacle, but that mysterious Presence I sensed had certainly triggered my reaction. Reflecting on this, I realized I had to know, at some level, what that Presence was. So I went back, and this time I made a beeline for the statue of Our Lady and, with difficulty, humbled myself to kneel before it.

I began attending Mass, and there I saw something different from anything I had experienced up to that point in Ithaca: ordinary people on their knees, pouring out their hearts in earnest prayer. But I was still scared of Jesus in the Blessed Sacrament —something it took a while to overcome—and, furthermore, summer was ending and my activist cohort was trickling back into town. When I excitedly began to share what had transpired in my soul that summer, their reaction was shock, horror, and incomprehension.

My resolve to become a Catholic began to waver. One Sunday I was lying on my bed, trying to decide whether to go to Mass. Finally I leaped up and sprinted to the church so as not to be late. But on the way, I realized I was wearing my ACT UP T-shirt (I belonged to the local chapter of the AIDS Coalition to Unleash Power). When I arrived, everyone was leaving—the parish had just shifted from its summer to its fall schedule—but in the vestibule stood a man handing out programs for an event that was about to occur: the Baptism of a child.

Nervously, I held out my hand for a program. The man looked at my T-shirt: jet-black with a huge pink triangle. But he gave me a program and motioned me in. At the Baptism of that child, whose name I do not remember, I was able and willing to recite the Baptismal Creed for the first time.

I was received into the Catholic Church at Easter in 1992, when I was twenty-three years old. So I've had more than half my lifetime since then to reflect on my situation. In October 2003, when *The Journey Home* very kindly hosted me, I was very confident that my past lay completely behind me. But I had underestimated the tenacity of my particular affliction, as well as the severity of what is known as the midlife crisis.

By God's grace, I have been celibate for twenty-four years. And as I mentioned on the program, through therapy and prayer, I (very unexpectedly) began to experience attraction to women. That is still present, but in recent years it has been swamped, I have to admit, by a tidal resurgence of homosexual lust.

Is this simply my thorn in the flesh — my cross to bear? Certainly, and in most ways it is no different from any of the crosses that direct us toward Heaven. But this one has certain troubling implications for my Christian journey.

First, in the current cultural climate, it makes me into an object lesson. I am, according to the dominant narrative, someone who came out into the light of "self-acceptance" but could not bear it and, out of fear, returned to the cave of "self-hatred." In truth, all it means is this: I have to affirm, against the grain, that the strength of a particular desire does not necessarily make that desire ethical.

I'm not alone in that, of course. Alcoholics have to confess that their most cherished desires are disordered and surrender them completely to a Higher Power. Until a few decades ago, nearly all psychologists understood that homosexuality, too, is disordered. But then homosexual behavior was manufactured into an identity and an ideology; it became a cause, and now anyone with same-sex attraction who has the humility to admit that there might be something wrong with him, based on his own compulsive and destructive acts, becomes a traitor to that cause and to our entire culture.

My moral struggles also had an effect on my inner life. I began to feel, once again, out of sync with the truth, the life, the reality that had attracted me to Christ and His Church. Joy, peace, and fulfillment in my religious life evaporated; my religious duties became rote habits rather than authentic worship. I did not lose the Faith; I still knew at the core of my being that all we believe as Catholics is true, but my heart was no longer engaged since it was preoccupied with my old longings. In short I became, not a hypocrite, but something of a practical atheist.

I was far from unique in this, as well; it's a common syndrome among nominal believers, but I found it unacceptable, and I grieved over my lack of love for God and my failure to live up to my Christian commitment inwardly, even though I still did so externally. In this way, practical atheism is in some ways the most virulent form of atheism; a true atheist is at least not a wolf in sheep's clothing, as I felt myself to be.

At times the only way I could conceptualize my faith was to think of myself as a captive in Christ's triumphal train—a willing captive, to be sure, since I freely acknowledged all His royal and divine prerogatives, but a captive nonetheless. And following my wandering heart, I at times made myself captive to sins I thought I had left behind long ago. If this was the dark night of the soul, I was flunking it. And, I felt, I was headed straight into the abyss.

Fortunately for me, this was not the dark night of the soul. A book given to me by a friend—one of the many male friends whom God in His generosity has bestowed on me—enabled me to name this new affliction: *The Noonday Devil: Acedia, the Unnamed Evil of Our Times* by Abbot Jean-Charles Nault.

Acedia featured in many of the original lists of deadly sins. This untranslatable Greek word was defined by St. Thomas Aquinas in a twofold way, both of which spoke to my condition: "Sadness about spiritual good"? Check. "Disgust with activity"? Check.

The root of acedia lies in the sufferer's reluctance to surrender some lesser good in order to pursue the highest good that is God. It often strikes in midlife, because that is when one loses patience with the lengthy slog toward Heaven and begins to long for the fleshpots of Egypt. The resulting spiritual sadness leaves the victim of acedia mired in a spiritual sloth that paralyzes all godly activity, draining it of joy and, at times, rendering it loathsome.

I felt immediate relief while reading Abbot Nault's book, especially upon learning that the treatment for acedia is simple and effective: contrition, work, prayer, perseverance, and meditation on death. But, above all, the medicine for acedia is *the Incarnation*. We grow weary of the spiritual life because we cannot see God in the Beatific Vision, but, as St. Thomas reassures us, the Incarnation proves that it is possible for our intellect to contemplate God.

And so I have turned to the Person of Christ, who took upon Himself every sinful condition and every darkness—and He meets us there. I now see acedia as a sharing in Christ's abandonment and His kenosis (self-emptying), and this experience helps me to realize that I can encounter Christ even through the unwanted suffering of same-sex attraction. My healing process continues, but I have begun to realize that the qualities God loves best in me are those which I have hated the most—the gentleness, the sensitivity, the compassion, and the intelligence that, given our society's insane definition of masculinity, left me vulnerable to the attribution of homosexuality.

More importantly, with the help of a twelve-step group, I now see that healing lies not in any good qualities I might have, but in honesty before God about my own defects, to which God responds with divine love and mercy. In short, I am beginning to understand that my discomfort on my awkward pilgrimage through the world, while an affliction, is actually what makes me a Christian.

I'm not out of the woods of acedia yet, but I now have a real and substantial hope, one far greater than all of my lesser hopes and desires.